Phil
from
Mary

Reydon Priory
Dec 1959 –

# I FORGOT TO TELL YOU

# I FORGOT
# TO TELL YOU

BY
L. E. JONES

RUPERT HART-DAVIS
SOHO SQUARE LONDON
1959

Made and printed in Great Britain by
William Clowes and Sons, Limited, London and Beccles

# I FORGOT TO TELL YOU

# CONTENTS

# 8 CONTENTS

## CHAPTER I

# MAN-SERVANT AND
# MAID-SERVANT

D URING his first four or five years the child of a
country squire in the reign of Queen Victoria
spent nine-tenths, if not more, of his waking
hours in the company of servants. It was from them
that he learnt the intricate business of eating, washing,
dressing and "behaving," with all their imposed rituals,
and it was to them that his natural affections first turned.

It is sad that the most deserving of them, the Nanny,
should have been so taken for granted as to leave the
faintest impression. That our own Emma Turner had
the devotion of her kind I know, but only from hearsay,
although I can recall a tranquil pleasure when she sang,
by the nursery fire, "Just a Song at Twilight." A more disturbing little ditty went as follows to a most plaintive air :

> The fire has gone out,
> The house is quite dark,
> And Mother is sitting alone,
> With poor brother Ben so sick on her lap,
> Oh father, dear father, come home!

"Sick," to us, did not mean ailing : it was the technical
word for vomiting, and I was horrified as well as moved
by the mother's plight and the father's disgust when, if
ever, he should return.

9

But Emma Turner, for the most part, has receded into the shadows, whereas Ethel, a schoolgirl of fourteen who came from the village as a temporary "help," I suppose, between nursery-maids, is still vivid in my mind's eye. For Ethel was a heroine, an ideal. She had long fair hair down to her shoulders, and a pair of enormous laced boots beneath her short skirts. Ethel would lean against a wall and cross one leg over the other, with only the toe of the crossed leg resting on the ground. This attitude gave her an air of noble insouciance, and I tried hard to imitate the tall girl. But with my short chubby legs I could not manage it; I merely fell over myself. I had to be content with looking forward to the day when I too, as I confided to all the maids, would have long fair hair and great laced boots and be called Ethel. For I was still at an age to have no sense of my own gender; I believed that I could grow up to be a man or a woman at will, and the sight of Ethel lolling against the wall and tapping that supercilious toe decided my choice. I wanted to be both beautiful and lordly.

In the sunny housekeeper's room I was Mrs Annell's little lamb and was given pink finger-biscuits, but in the stable-yard I was Coachman's little lamb as well, and this joint ownership rather puzzled and confused me, until Mrs Annell disappeared overnight. Mrs Annell was Scotch: when my mother told her to put away her wedding-dress Mrs Annell had it dyed black and wore it in church, for it seems that in her part of Scotland "put away" meant "throw away," which Mrs Annell justly felt would be a pity. Because she was dressed in black and wore an immense round lace cap with ribbons on it I believed her to be very old; but in fact she was young enough, as I learnt for the first time sixty-five years later, to be caught *in flagrante delicto* with a butler, and in consequence had to leave us by a very early train indeed. Thereafter Coachman had his little lamb all to himself.

But Coachman, who refused to tell us why he sported a cockade on the side of his top-hat, saying that we should know when we were older (which made me suppose cockades to be somehow connected with death), was soon outshone in his own stable yard by Jim, the groom. Although Jim's favourite hymn was "Every Morning the Red Sun" while mine was "Hark, Hark my Soul," this difference in our outlooks did not affect my hero-worship. Jim's forearms, when he was cleaning harness, were fascinating; they had little black hairs on them because, the maids told us, he was so strong. (Another manservant had beads of water on his forehead when he put our Cromer portmanteaux on to the luggage cart because, the maids told us, he was not strong.) When we met Jim in the park one day he took off his cap with a great sweep and behold! it was lined with early primroses. A very pretty trick, I thought; and, falling behind to visit the hedge-sparrow's nest in the box-hedge by the bees, I placed the four blue eggs in my own hat, settled it firmly on my head and marched up to the nursery. But when I swept it off with what I believed to be Jim's easy gesture, I got no applause. We had shock-heads in those days, and the nursery-maid was not only rude but rough as she held mine under the tap.

Our nursery-maids were generally called Alice, and on the whole I think we were lucky in them, although personally I had a strong objection, of which I made no secret when they knelt on the mat to dry me after a bath, to the way in which their chests stuck out. "I would like to cut you down straight," I would tell them, while they protested that it was not their fault that they were made to bulge so annoyingly. But there was one Alice who not only pronounced "butter" as "batter," but who slipped up on our newt, and broke all the tea-things. How our newt climbed out of the glass aquarium he shared with the stickleback and the minnow I cannot imagine, but escape he did and was transformed by Alice's slither into a long, glistening green streak on the linoleum. We were shocked and nauseated, but, with the objectivity of the very young, fascinated by the enormous length to which a newt can be extended by the weight of a nursery-maid. It was a matter of yards.

Nursery-maids came and went, the nicest Alices leaving us "to better themselves," an objective of which I was never able to form a very clear conception. Why should they become better Alices away from us all? Fortunately, Nelly Bayliss remained. Nelly had been second nurse under Emma Turner, and when Emma had to depart in tears, because unable to cope with my three-year-old next-younger brother, Nelly stepped into her shoes.

Master Bertram had painted the inside of the bath with Mr Priest's paints; he had refused to kiss Mr Priest as an apology, because Mr Priest's beard was prickly; he had cut off most of his hair "to look like Jim"; he had mown down the tulips in the square garden; and it was felt that black-haired Nelly, who would stand no nonsense, must relieve the gentle, loving Emma. But it was as second nurse, before her sobering days of responsibility, that Nelly comes most vividly back to me. And not, I am glad to say, as the Nelly we "hated," when she ran us down the passage, after some mis-behaviour at table, alternately knocking our heads forward with her knuckles and jerking them backwards by the hair, but as the glorious entertainer. For at one end of the day-nursery there was an enormous maho-gany dais, which in my grandfather's day had encased a bath, and, when our parents were safely at Schwalbach or Mentone, Nelly would mount upon this eminence, dressed in the footman's trousers, to sing, dance and play upon her concertina. Alas, I cannot remember her songs, except for one that began:

> The Prince of Wales was Chairman,
> Of course he opened the Ball,
> And sang the chorus of every song
> In the concert at Albert Hall.

and "The Roast Beef of Old England." She also danced a most spirited hornpipe. For all their directness, small children are capable of living double lives, and we never reported these most enjoyable affairs to our parents. We instinctively felt that my mother would not have been amused by Nelly's trousers; and indeed, when in after years we talked of these goings-on, my mother said we must have dreamt it. Nothing of the sort could ever have been permitted by her exemplary domestics. But my mother was a good deal shaken a few years later when she came unexpectedly into the nursery to find Nelly, now head-nurse, reading aloud to us from a most delectable book called *Herr Baby*. We adored it, but there was a painful scene, for my mother confiscated it on the spot, telling Nelly that it was as bad as reading a

novel to us. "A novel"—we had no idea what a novel
might be, and for years the word was associated in my
mind with something unspeakable.

Nelly had an aunt at Little Walsingham, with whom
we sometimes went to tea. Much as we disliked the
pony-cart, this was a notable treat, for Nelly's aunt,
who wore a black bonnet, not only lived among the
ruins of an ancient friary, with little stone staircases that
led nowhere, but fed us with miniature hot buttered
scones, about the size of half a crown. They were heaped
up into a kind of pyramid in the middle of Nelly's
aunt's tea-table and, unlike most delicacies, there were
more than we could eat. How vivid, how ineluctable,
are memories of food! Nelly's aunt, the provider, has,
but for her black bonnet, vanished altogether.

Even the drive to Walsingham had its excitements,
for by a very small detour we could pass beneath the
great dark, leafy tunnel of Chestnut Grove at West
Barsham, and pull up at the end of it to watch the black-
smith at his anvil. And further on there was the Slipper
Chapel, where the pilgrims to the shrine of Our Lady
at Walsingham used to leave their shoes behind and
walk the last mile barefoot. We never tired of Nelly's
story of the two pilgrims who, for a penance, had been
ordered to walk to Walsingham with peas in their
boots. One hobbled painfully and in great distress, but
the other strode ahead, singing joyfully: he had boiled
the peas before stuffing them into his shoes. We thought
this a master-stroke, as indeed it was. Very different
were our feelings about our drives to East Rudham as
escorts to "Aggie's bad hand." Aggie was a laundry-
maid, and her bad hand, in which a needle had been
lost, was an affliction to us as well as to Aggie. For there

cannot be a duller road than the Rudham road, and
Aggie, who held aloft a lumpy and shapeless bandage
in our midst, was very poor company. We had to be
careful of Aggie's bad hand all the way, and the long
wait outside Dr Rowell's surgery, while the lost needle
was being hunted, was a trial to our patience. I am afraid
poor Aggie must have suffered a good deal, to judge
from the indelible mark that her bad hand has made
upon my mind. It recalls not an incident but rather an
epoch; an interlude of dreariness and monotony, of an
endless road between low dusty hedges, a road made
still more distasteful by memories of a bygone, but
frightening, encounter with "the loose horses." I hope
we were sorry for Aggie, but, if so, I have forgotten it.
I know we were more than sorry for ourselves.

Because our mother was also our governess, there was
no sudden transition in our lives from nursery to schoolroom. We sat at the same table with the nurse, nursery-
maid and younger children from the time when we
believed the curled feather which lay on the floor by
one of Landseer's hounds to be "his Sunday tail" to the
day when we christened the mother-cat in the big
oleograph "Marathon," and her three kittens "Thermopylae," "Salamis" and "Plataea." (The black one was
Thermopylae, the lost battle.) I forget if this was the
occasion of Sarah the cook's emphatic declaration that
she thanked Heaven she had not been born a little lady
because of the intolerable burden of book-learning laid
upon such. But book-learning was undoubtedly the
barrier which was gradually lowered to divide us from
our cronies of the pantry, the kitchen, the laundry and
the stable-yard. From humble and engrossed admirers
of the strength and skill of our daily companions we

imperceptibly changed into smug, if puny, school-inspectors. We discovered that Nausicaa meant nothing to the laundry-maids, Bellerophon nothing to Coachman. Instead of listening and learning, we began to tell them things. And in the kindness of their hearts, they pretended to be impressed and even astonished by the things we told them. The old natural relationship between curious child and capable adult was upset; a smattering of knowledge coupled, it is only fair to say, with a stimulated imagination was beginning to take the upper hand of the untaught and the unreflective. I do not know whether the rest of the servants would have agreed with Sarah in her thankfulness for being spared the burden of education, but I am inclined to think they would. Dockerell, the butler, did have a wistful moment of wishing he knew French after seeing us act scenes from *Le Bourgeois Gentilhomme*, but nobody would have been more astonished than Dockerell could he have seen, forty years later, a successor, Mr Wheeler, reading Schopenhauer in his pantry. Astonished and, I am inclined to think, disapproving. He would have felt that the silver must suffer.

I have no experience of how, in other Victorian families like ours, the transition from social intimacy between children and servants to the full-blown "master and man" relationship was managed. For our faintly patronising ways with the maids had not, from our side at least, cast any shadow over kitchen and back-passage gossip when, in my eleventh year, my family went abroad. And there the domestic fabric was of another pattern altogether. For one thing, the maids and Auguste, the moon-faced man-of-all-work, talked much better French than we did. There was no coming it over them with scraps from Molière. Nor did they wear caps or livery. They had perfect manners, but expected to be listened to when they argued, for which purpose they had an extensive vocabulary. They "knew their place" as precisely as any English servant, but in a different sense, for "their place" was to see that the family was properly looked after, and if, to achieve this, it was necessary to contradict their master or mistress flat, contradict them they did. Nor had our elderly cook Louise—a *cordon bleu* within her own limits— anything in common with our good Sarah. Louise pounded and seethed and simmered her materials many hours, even days, before they came to table; she used "weeds" such as dandelion-leaves and young nettles, and would have used most of the toadstools had we not, in our insular ignorance, jibbed; she subscribed for a financial paper in which to study the ups and downs of her *placements*. She was little and ageless and peasant-like, but our richest friend from the smart world of the Californie at Cannes would make greedy noises and ask for more of one of Louise's soufflés or ragoûts. With Auguste we went fishing, and learnt about Morocco and the hard life of a conscript.

So there was no more patronising or holding of *viva voce* examinations, and our next contact with English maids was with the Eton boys' maids. These hard-working creatures served us but were not our servants; they were even under an obligation, in some circum-stances, to report us to the house-tutor; the relationship could very easily have become an uncomfortable one. But in my own experience it never did. To small boys a boys' maid like our own Cox could be a real comfort, for Cox's judgment of individuals was unclouded by

2

the faintest regard for athletic or social success. I remember my astonishment at hearing from Cox that a boy who had left just before I arrived, a boy without colours or any kind of distinction in the school at large, had been "the light of the 'ouse" to her. As I grew to know Cox better, I felt that that boy must have had enviable qualities. We laughed at Cox for calling prunes "pruings," but appreciated her, especially when we were nobodies, for being no respecter of persons. In appearance she looked a little like Miss Flora Robson, and it may be that my warm feelings for that accomplished actress (whom I have never met) are partly based on a subconscious association of ideas.

If boys' maids are in a class apart, so are college scouts, their masculine counterparts at Oxford, with whom I next had to do. They, too, served, but owed no obedience to, the men on their staircases, and our commerce with them was accordingly good training in the art, not always understood by the young and brash, of dealing with other people's servants in other people's houses. To get things done for you without giving orders, to accept service neither as master nor supplicant, are social acquirements that are not ready-made to hand, especially for the shy. The scouts were our 'nets,' where we could try out our strokes before playing the game on country-house visits. My own scout, Turner, was a grizzled veteran without any graces and considerable powers of disapproval, but he watched over our basic comforts faithfully and well. Our water was hot, our breakfasts punctual and our fires did not go out. He could be glum, but his attitude was protective; we were his charges, not his bosses, and, once that was understood, he was anxious to oblige us. His wintry smile of welcome at the beginning of a new term was genuine. Perhaps I learnt from Turner that the most intimidating of butlers, in the grandest of houses, could be tamed if you put yourself under his wing.

Today butlers are a dying species, almost extinct, and I see nothing to regret in their disappearance. I have always felt that the versatility, the self-command and self-effacement, the resourcefulness, the impassivity, the devotion of these remarkable men was wasted in the service of a single family. Theirs should have been wider spheres, and I have little doubt but that today our armed forces, Civil Service and industries are the better for the presence of thousands of formidable personalities who, but for our social revolution, would have been butlers. And there is another comforting thought. Never again will there be such a master-and-servant relationship as that which prompted Hearne, the Victorian butler of the Amhersts at Didlington Hall, to respond to my mother's murmured condolences on the death of his wife with: "It is of no consequence at all, my lady." Were ever more truly dreadful words of reassurance spoken by a broken-hearted man? I prefer to remember another, temporary, butler at Didlington, whose habit it was, before replenishing your glass, to say, "*More* champagne, sir?" in a hollow tone of infinite reproach. It needed courage indeed to say "Please."

But if I cannot regret their passing as a class, that is not to say that I do not have grateful memories of many of these gifted men. Who was ever more welcoming or more protective to youthful guests than Howes at Munstead? What more flattering audience for my stories than Artis at Buckhurst—Artis whose twinkling eye behind the chairs it was my ambition to catch? Who more friendly and versatile than Edwards at Westonbirt? Who more silently serviceable than Collier at Lochluichart? And if Mrs Pheby at Glenlochay did not claim the name of butler, no manservant was ever more competent, authoritative and stately than that tall, warm-hearted head-servant, who stood so regally on the doorstep to welcome a guest.

From where did butlers come? I have never seen a footman with the faintest air of being a potential butler, just as, in the Army, I never saw a Brigadier who could have been mistaken for a Major-General. I have known statesmen and editors who resembled butlers; I recall a boy at Eton who was even known as "the butler." I have seen, in butlers, many outward marks of statesmen. But never have I set eyes on an obvious, unmistakable, budding butler. Their provenance remains a mystery.

My acquiescence in life without butlers does not mean that I am equally unconcerned over the dearth of maid-servants. The work of a parlour-maid seems to me to be more varied, responsible and interesting than machine-minding or typing, or than most of the monotonous and repetitive activities in factories and workshops. To tempt young women back into our homes we shall have to give up calling them "Alice" on first acquaintance, and capping them with badges of servitude. Nor must their hours of work be dependent upon their employers' fitfulness. But if the status now given to typists and receptionists were to be accorded to her, and a high standard of skill demanded from her, I cannot see why Miss Smith should not be glad to spend

some years in a profession which will do far more to
fit her for a home of her own than any other job. If
"esteem" is the element hitherto lacking in domestic
service, it is up to us to supply it. How willingly, how
highly, how genuinely would most harassed housewives
esteem any Miss Smith prepared to give her skilled
assistance! Had our own Lucy Smith, many years ago,
enjoyed the kind of status I have in mind, she might
not have been tempted to practise those deceits which
caused so much heart-burning to a young Australian
officer. Lucy was a pretty, drooping creature, inefficient
and lackadaisical, whom one would have judged to be
incapable of saying "Bo" to the least of her fellow-
geese. But to the Australian officer she was Miss Smythe,
living, since her father in the Guards had been killed
out hunting and her mother had re-married, as companion to a Lady Evelyn Jones in London. They became
engaged, but the Australian received a disturbing letter
from a Mrs Smith in Essex. It was ill-written and ill-
spelt, but it purported to come from Miss Lucy Smythe's
mama, the widow of the Guards officer. Did her
daughter's fiancé understand that Lucy came from a
cottage home and was in service as a parlour-maid?
The distracted fiancé sent the letter on to my wife. He
was indifferent to his pretty Lucy's birth, but very much
concerned with her honesty. So poor Lucy, who had
felt herself obliged by lack of status to tell whoppers,
lost her Australian.

Today, when I am myself a part-time parlour-maid,
housemaid, scullery-maid and valet, I find that, on the
whole, I esteem myself more, and not less, for my part
in those employments, and have felt no loss of status.
It is true that I am under nobody's orders, but if it is

fear of the master-and-servant nexus that is keeping the young women out of our homes, there is surely a way round. A professional who knows her business should be able to give her services as a matter of contract, and to regard her former masters as customers or clients, people who must be pleased, but not obeyed. Or, better still, let her regard herself, as William did, as the helper of the helpless.

William was a little wisp of a man, meagre, emaciated and untidy, who was in charge of our own and our two elder daughters' service flats in Pall Mall. He had a small wizened face, watery eyes, scant hair, few words and a shambling walk. His normal expression was downcast and dreary; he mumbled when he spoke; he slunk about Crown Passage furtively in a dusty bowler hat. Apart from appearing to be such a starveling that no Christian would ask him to carry a tray, let alone a suitcase, he wore an air of melancholy and misanthropy which was most unpromising. His bedroom, into which I once had a horrified glance, was a narrow, gloomy, passage-like room, almost entirely blocked by coat-and-trouser hangers. My heart sank when I first saw William.

In fact he was a treasure. Formally he was the landlord's and not our servant, but it made no matter; William, as I have said, regarded himself as the helper of the helpless. He adopted us. Our lives ran smoothly, our comforts were assured, by the noiseless attentions of this untidy waif. He even managed a smile for us, a crooked, fleeting smile which disclosed one lonely upper tooth. William, as far as I could make out, had no family. He never took a holiday. I pressed him to come and rest in Norfolk, hoping to fatten him, but he would not. Crown Passage, and its cosy Red Lion, could not, in William's opinion, be bettered, and for family, had he not his helpless charges?

When, after we had quitted Pall Mall, the flats were bombed, I felt anxious for William; he was not among the killed, but might not so frail a featherweight have been blown away? And how was so unpresentable, so dilapidated a little creature to find fresh employment? I went to make enquiries. I need not have worried. William was still haunting Crown Passage. His crooked one-tooth smile was still there. He had found employment in a club.

In the seventeenth chapter of St Luke's Gospel we are told how Jesus, talking to his disciples, took it for granted that they were slave-owners who would expect a slave of theirs, coming in exhausted from the plough, to wait unrefreshed at his master's table before getting his own supper. From the days of Jesus until the Second World War this was the common assumption of masters and servants alike. It is no longer so. Did Jehovah, when delivering law to Moses on Sinai, foresee that in three thousand years the language of the fourth commandment would be obsolete? Any day now, some child at his mother's knee may well ask: "What does man-servant and maid-servant mean, Mummy?"

## CHAPTER II

# ONLY A GAME

FEW men can ever have meant better by their children than did my father. Being unoccupied for the last sixty of his ninety-seven years, he had plenty of time on hand for making plans for our benefit, but he was impulsive, and did not always pause to consider the beneficiary's point of view. On one occasion a bright idea of my father's, acted upon without consulting myself, caused me to suffer a measure of anxiety and humiliation that left a scar for years.

I was thirteen at the time and had been already two halves at Eton. Owing to the death from pneumonia, at the beginning of the summer holidays, of an elder brother from whom I had never been separated, it was decided that I should not return to Eton for the ensuing half, but go instead to learn French in Paris. The Fashoda incident, however, and the momentary belligerence of the French caused my father, after buying an evening paper on Dover pier, to change his mind, and the family, having no English home, went into lodgings at Westgate-on-Sea, there to wait upon events.

There was, in those days, a private school at Westgate kept by a burly, red-faced clergyman called Mr Bull, with whom my father had some slight acquaintance. The sight of Mr Bull's boys playing football on the other side of some iron railings put into my father's head the bright idea which cost me so much. Without consulting me, he called upon Mr Bull, reminded him of a meeting many years ago at Cambridge or Schwalbach or wherever else, and asked him whether his lonely Eton boy might join Mr Bull's boys for a game of football. Mr Bull said he might; let the boy report to the Games Master on the football field the following afternoon.

My father returned to our lodging in high feather, and told me the good news. I was horrified. I had never played football in my life, nor even kicked a football since childhood days. I, too, had looked through those iron railings, and watched the intricate manœuvring, the curious waiting about combined with sudden darts and gyrations of soccer-players, and saw at a glance that it would be impossible for me, wholly uninstructed, to walk on to that field and "play football." I protested, pleading that I did not know how to play football. "Not play football? A strong, active boy like you! Of course you can play football."

My father swept all my objections aside. He had no intention of allowing his own bright idea, and his old friend Bull's "kindness," to go for nothing. I had only to do as the other boys did. I should enjoy it enormously. Nothing of the parson about Bull. He couldn't have been nicer. Shorts? Only little boys wear shorts. Had I not my knickerbockers and a jersey? Brown boots would do perfectly.

Had I been a little older, I might have reminded my father of his habit of deriding both private schools and organised games. Had my mother not been so grief-stricken, I might have called in aid an ally to whom my father invariably gave in. As it was, spiritless and panic-stricken, I lived over in imagination the dreadful hour that was to come.

On the following day I put on my grey flannel knickerbockers, my white jersey and my brown walking-boots with slightly pointed toes, and walked down to the school. The little boys were already gathering into groups on the beastly field. They all wore shorts, stockings with coloured tops, and football-boots with square toes and strips of leather across the soles to prevent slipping. As I walked towards them across the grass I realised for the first time that I was a giant, towering above a race of pygmies, but an awkward stick of a giant. My knickerbockers among all those bare knees gave me a curious feeling of being slightly effeminate, such as a young priest might have when first walking in a cassock among a crowd of men in trousers. My smooth soles felt insecure on the wet grass, speckled with worm-casts.

The Games Master, with a ball under one arm and a whistle round his neck, was reading out names from a piece of paper. He was the first games master I had seen; he wore a Norfolk jacket and an enormous woollen scarf and looked healthier than seemed quite human. He appeared to be surprised as I approached him; it was clear that Mr Bull had forgotten to tell him about me; and my ordeal was aggravated at the very start by the unforeseen necessity of explaining myself. The pygmies stared, with small upturned faces. The Games Master, unsmilingly, asked me at what position I usually played. I told him I had never played. It took him some time to take this in, and I murmured something about being at Eton, in the despairing hope, I suppose, that he might think I was all right at the Eton game. In the end he decided to put me in Bunny's side as an extra half-back. I had no idea what a half-back might be.

I have made, in later life, a friend called Bunny, to whom I am grateful, among much else, for his having finally exorcised the nightmare association with which that trivial nickname had been, for most of my life, made odious to me. Not that there was anything hateful about Bunny himself. He was a very short, stocky little boy with a freckled face and two little peeping front teeth which must have earned him his soubriquet. As captain of my side he took no notice of me whatsoever. But if ever I have been humiliated beyond bearing it was by Bunny. For Bunny was a prodigy of skill at soccer. One of the smallest boys in the game, he dominated it. "Well done, Bunny!" "Well kicked, Bunny!" "Shoot, Bunny!" and Bunny shot, and into the goal went the ball. I, in contrast to Bunny, was staggering about in hopeless confusion. On the few occasions when the ball came to me, I kicked it as hard as I could in the direction of the opposing goal, thereby upsetting any plan that was afoot. I could not recognise friend from foe. I knew nothing of passing. I was always getting in the way. And round me, and across me, and behind me, Bunny darted and leapt, intercepting, dodging, tackling, dribbling, passing and shooting, with the Games Master shouting approval and praise. I seemed to get taller and taller, more and more con-spicuous, as I blundered about. I felt a fool and knew I must be looking one. If only someone had laughed at me, so that I could have laughed with him; if only the Games Master had suggested that I should drop out and try to learn something from the side-line! But football was clearly no laughing matter at Bull's; I was surrounded with serious, intent and contemptuous little faces. It was hellish, and it went on for an hour.

I have no recollection of saying good-bye to Bunny or the Games Master, or of thanking them for my nice game, but I suppose I must have said something. Nor do I remember making any report to my father. If I did so, I probably said it was "quite fun." Humiliation was the very last thing I should ever have confessed to. But my father did not suggest another game. Perhaps Mr Bull gave him a hint.

How pleasant it is to grow up; to achieve some sort of athletic success; to develop a sense of humour; to be able to find fun in being a fish out of water. My next adventure as an outsider among experts was when I played, a lubberly wet-bob, for I Zingari. It was a wholly delightful experience. There was a cricket week at Brympton in Somerset, the home of the Ponsonby-Fanes. The Brympton eleven were to play an I Zingari side at Montacute, where I was staying. The Zingari found themselves short of two players, and young Francis Lascelles and myself were raked in to make up the number. I played, in grey flannels and brown tennis-shoes, among the immaculate white trousers and whiter cricket-boots, without a qualm. It had rained all night, but a hot sun came out and made the drying wicket exceedingly sticky. We batted first, and one after another the good cricketers were defeated by the spin bowlers, albeit in the most stylish manner, for under fifty runs. Lascelles and I naturally batted last. We were too ignorant to know about the treachery of the wicket. We were enchanted to have slow bowlers to deal with, for a fast bowler, however indifferent, is sudden death to a wet-bob. We leapt down the pitch and slogged at

every ball. We ran between the wickets like hares.
Together we added over thirty runs to the score. I made
twenty-two not out, the highest score. The fielding side
were disgusted. "This nonsense must stop!" shouted
one of them. Bearded Dick Ponsonby-Fane, who kept
wicket, looked more haggard than ever. Even our own
side disapproved of the performance. Not a clap did we
get when we eventually came out together; not one
word, even of jocular congratulation, was said to the
beaming top-scorer. "Not cricket" was the general
verdict. I am afraid Lascelles and I had laughed and
shouted as we ran, and generally upset the decorum of
the most solemn and sacred of all games. But none of
this could depress us. We were outsiders, who had taken
no vows and made no submission to a Grave Rule. It
was a glorious quarter of an hour. It would have been
more glorious still if the captain of our side, so pained,
so embarrassed, had been called Bunny.

## CHAPTER III

# THE APOLOGY

I AM not sure that I have ever quite recovered from it, although to anyone but myself the affair must appear almost laughably slight. But to an Etonian, seventeen years old if not more, already a member of the Eight, and approaching, in his own eyes, the last lap of adolescence, it was a shocking experience. Shocking, because it made me feel—although I should not, of course, have so put it at the time—that a large part of my life had been wasted, had been lived to no purpose, since here I was once again, in a flash as it were, reduced to mere childhood, to the status of a little, naughty boy. And the reduction was so sudden, my new plight so abject, that I had little power of resistance. All that imagined maturity of my life at Eton, of the Captain of House, the master of fags, the owner of a razor, suddenly collapsed; I could not call it in aid, could not produce my testimonials, because my behaviour had proved all that ripeness to be nugatory and invalid. Proved it, at least to my mother, if not to myself, and it was my mother's opinion that counted. From my mother's decisions, on questions of conduct, there was no appeal, not even to conscience. She could undo, in a moment, what it had taken years to build up; she could take away our characters; reduce us to the ranks; and destroy our pasts.

It happened in the Easter holidays, on the Valescure golf course and a lovely morning. My father, Colonel Call and myself were playing a three-ball match, and my mother was walking round the course with us. On a certain green my father had a short putt for the hole. He fluffed his putt, and the ball was rolling to one side when my father stretched out his putter and stroked the ball into the hole, saying, "All square," or whatever the score would have been had he holed the putt. Instead of laughing, as the Colonel laughed, at my father's bare-faced impudence, I went red in the face and exclaimed: "That's cheating!"

I do not remember my father's reaction. He probably said, "Nonsense! we're playing for fun," or something of the sort, and would have forgotten it. But my mother turned to stone upon the green. Because the Colonel was there, she said nothing. She merely moved away, rigid and stricken. There were a few more holes to play. The Colonel did his best to be chatty and un- concerned, but the game was ruined. And not only the game. So strong was my mother's personality, so chil- ling the emanations of her disapproval, that for me, if not for the Colonel and my father, the bright day itself, the stone pines, the distant Ste Baume, the myrtle and the cistus, were at one swift stroke bereft of virtue.

I do not remember how I got through the rest of that day. I was too big to be scolded: but I was outlawed. My mother did not speak to me; her eyes never met my own; I was ignored by her. To say that our family lived by the warmth of my mother's approval, as the earth by the sun's, is not to put it too high. The wispiest, most fugitive of clouds between her and any member of the family affected us all. And when the cloud remained for long impenetrable, as on the occasion I am recalling, everybody was miserable.

There was nothing calculated, nothing deliberately punitive, in these self-eclipses of our light-giver. My mother had no guile; she was incapable of pretence. That any child of hers should have loudly accused his father of cheating, and before a stranger, was an occasion for, not anger, but stony, desolating grief. And hide it she could not. The surprising thing, in retrospect, is that I held out so long. I was no longer a child; I ought to have known that a golfer who cheats does so out of sight, in a bunker or in the rough; he hopes to deceive. My father's action had been one of gay and open defiance, a refusal to be bound by mere rules. The putt was a short one and the ball ought to have rolled in without that added boost—besides, he had given it the merest touch, nothing that could be called, or counted as, a "stroke." In after years, at family bridge, I grew accustomed to seeing my father gather up all the hands from the table and deal afresh if he had happened to deal himself a Yarborough. He played all games for the fun of winning, and a bad hand or a missed putt spoilt that fun; so he took steps to correct any flaw in his enjoyment. It was the same with his favourite Metternich patience. If the game refused to come out, he would change a card until it did, and was not a whit the less pleased with a triumphant ending. But for some reason I felt stubborn and unrepentant about my impulsive and erroneous cry of "Cheating!" I was aggrieved both by my father's contempt for the rules and by my mother's reaction to it. I persuaded myself that I, as a stickler for the rigour of the game, had the right of it; that my father had let down the family in

the eyes of the Colonel, and that my mother, so far
from blaming me, should herself have told my father
that he really could not do a thing like that. So I held
out, in spite of the general discomfort, for, I believe, a
second day—a second day of grim and chilly self-
righteousness.

Of course it could only end in one way, and in
complete surrender. I made the approach; my mother
drew a picture of my conduct that appalled me; I made
abject submission, and we were reconciled. But upon
terms; and it was the performance of those terms, simple
and obvious as they were, that I still remember with a
twinge of undeserved self-pity. Apologising to my
father cost me nothing. For all his Celtic excitability he
was the sweetest-tempered man I have ever known, and
could not bear malice for two minutes together. But
the article of my submission which, being totally unexpected, horrified me, was the stipulation that I must
seek out the Colonel and tell him that I was ashamed of
myself. So tremulous, so seasick did it make me feel,
that I even pleaded to be let off. But my mother was
adamant. I had disgraced myself before the Colonel,
and to the Colonel I must confess my shame.

It was not that the Colonel himself was an alarming
person. On the contrary, Colonel Call, who had so far
departed from military tradition as to grow a soft,
pointed beard in his retirement, was the gentlest and
most courteous of men. But there was this about him
which made him the last of the grown-up members of
our English colony before whom I could wish to stand
in a white sheet: he had taken an extraordinary fancy
to my younger brother and to myself. Every little
detail of our careers, in the Navy and at Eton, interested

him; he was forever sympathising or congratulating and showing interest; and for several years now he had treated me as a young man, rational and adult. To some of my father's casual golfing-partners I could have gone, unwillingly but not unbearably, to play the repentant schoolboy obeying his Mama. But to the Colonel, who found me so sensible, so mature! To go to him to confess myself a fraud, a silly, unmannerly little boy! No, it was not to be borne. Yet do it I must.

It is the stomach, not the head, that is affected by ordeals of this kind. Mine certainly, like the mind of Dr Johnson's female lodger, was all wiggle-waggle as I got out my bicycle, and, indeed, there were more risks than one to be faced. Those were the days before private telephones, and I had no means of making an appointment with the Colonel. I must take my chance, and the chances seemed to me in favour of my first meeting with Mrs Call, who seldom left the house. Now Mrs Call, although always friendly, was a formidable character. She was a daughter of Shelley's Trelawny, whose portrait, in fez and Greek dress, festooned with pistols and scimitars, hung in the drawing-room of the Villa Call, and she had inherited that adventurer's spirit and unconventionality. Also she was stone-deaf. Should I meet her first, she would ask me my business, and hand me a pencil and writing-pad for my reply. Was I to write upon that pad: "Because I called my father a cheat on the golf-course?" I could hear her derisive laughter, and her probable comment, "Well, why not, if he cheated?" So as I bicycled down the dusty white road between the pines, past the Villa Nelson, past the Villa Suveret, past the Hôtel D'Angleterre, I wished it might have been up-, not down-hill.

The Villa Call was a complete Surrey villa. Red brick
and gabled, it might have been lifted entire from
Camberley. The Colonel had built it himself, and his
instructions to his architect must have been: "No con-
cessions to blue skies, to Provence, to the ancient
traditions of the Mediterranean. Be British!" I suppose
I must have heard my parents' amused comments; for
even in my torment I was aware, as I turned in at the
narrow drive, that the Colonel lived in a stuffier atmosphere than ours, and might well regard my errand as
an embarrassing symptom of my parents' eccentricity.
By the time I had rung the door-bell I was near to
dithering on behalf of the Joneses at large.

But all went well. I asked for the Colonel, and
although I was shown into the drawing-room, where
Trelawny's long lank moustaches and fancy dress
contrasted strangely with the Surrey interior, Mrs Call
did not appear. I rushed my fence, gulped out the word
"ashamed," was patted on the back and told not to give
it another thought, and even detected in the Colonel's
benign eye a glint of fellow-feeling. Had he, too, felt
that my father's win at that hole had not been quite
golf? It comforted me to think so. As I pushed my
bicycle back up the long hill I felt hungry again for the
first time in forty-eight hours. I had done penance, at a
great cost; but had I truly repented? I am not sure.
Had I done so, would the memory of that ordeal be
still so vivid? My mother's forgiveness was, as ever,
absolute, leaving no mark on her loving mind. Why
was a mark left upon my own? I had a fright, as I have
said, at finding that a sudden fall from grace could undo
all my past. Or was the real shock, the sharp edge of the
affair which cut a still discernible notch upon my

experience, the discovery that my store of accumulated merit was at the mercy of another man's vagaries? I am sure that my mother persuaded me that my cry of "Cheating!" had been indefensible. But whereas a true penitent rejects all thoughts of excuse or provocation, there lingered with me and still lingers a faint sense of aggrievement. My father ought not, with however light a heart, on however fine a morning, to have nudged that ball into the hole.

## CHAPTER IV

# BELIEVE IT OR NOT

O N the things of which I am about to tell that took place one summer's day on Dartmoor, I have but one comment to make: that they happened. I can offer no explanation of them, nor can they be linked, except through the personality of B, with those other so-called "psychic" phenomena which have brought to me, as to many others, satisfactory evidence of our survival of bodily death.

The girl whom I shall call B. was the younger sister of one of my school-fellows. Her family was of good, solid stock, very English, intelligent but not imaginative, and decidedly conventional in all their ways. They lived in a spacious old house in an old London square; they were regular church-goers; they had not, when I first knew them, had any acquaintance with, or taken the slightest interest in, the practice or the literature of what is known as "psychical research." They would have dismissed all talk of such things as spooky nonsense.

The eldest girl of three, B. was, at seventeen or eighteen, an attractive, well-educated creature, of rather downright speech and with a few remnants of the schoolroom's uncertain manners. She was candid, un-complicated and matter-of-fact. She was also, as events were to prove, uncommonly fearless. To those who knew her, any suspicion of deceit in B. was not to be thought of. Her integrity was unassailable.

I was staying, one summer, with B.'s family on Dartmoor. It was decided to picnic on one of the Tors. The party drifted away from the house loosely, in twos and threes, each group taking its own line among the valley's bogs and rushes, and thereafter picking separate sheep-tracks through the warm, pervasive heather. I was walking with B. and Mrs X, a young married woman who has read and confirmed this account of what happened. For some reason we had lagged behind the others. There are two points to bear in mind about B. that morning: she wore a white blouse with short sleeves that ended in a frill well above the elbow, and in her right hand she carried an alpenstock.

The morning was already hot; we climbed lazily enough towards the first of several false crests that hid our Tor, and the rest of the party was out of sight when B.'s alpenstock fell from her outstretched right hand and rattled on the path. She was a pace or two in front of me, and I saw the alpenstock fall; but B., instead of stooping to pick it up, gave a surprised yelp and stood still with her right arm stretched out as before. I stepped up to her and saw that her face was contorted with pain; there were tears in her eyes. She turned and held her right arm towards me. "Cramp," she said; "it's agony." Her right fist was tightly clenched. I took her forearm and began to massage it. It felt like a table-leg, hard and unyielding. "Try my fist," she said. Those who have suffered from cramp will know, as I did, what torture B. was undergoing. I tried to open her fist. I have never yet met a man strong enough to keep his fist closed against me if I take each finger separately and

force it upwards and backwards. I tried this dodge, but
it was no good. B.'s fingers remained clamped against
her palm. Fist and forearm alike seemed to be made of
steel. Then suddenly, while I was still working desperately at her fingers, relief came. The fingers went soft
and slack in my own. B. moaned with relief and opened
her hand. In the palm lay an old-fashioned brooch, in
the shape of a peacock's feather, set with green and blue
stones of which several were missing. It had a tarnished,
shabby look.

"Mother's old brooch," said B. "She lost it some-
where in London at least six months ago!"

But that was only the beginning. We three turned up
the hill again. Soon B. stopped and said: "Somebody's
calling you—from over there." She pointed to the right,
away from our path. I had heard and could hear nothing.

"It's a man calling your name."

We waited a few seconds.

"There he is," said B., pointing again. I saw nothing
but the heather and a couple of Dartmoor ponies
grazing. The crest towards which B. pointed was not
more than a couple of hundred yards away. She left
the path and walked in that direction. When she had
gone about forty yards she turned and called to us:
"It's Archie Gordon."

Archie Gordon had died about eight months earlier
from injuries received in a motor-accident. B. scarcely
knew him, but had met him at an Oxford Commemora-
tion Ball. He had been a close friend of Mrs X. and
myself. B. went a little further into the heather, and we
followed. She was speaking, and stretching out her
hands, moving this way and that. "He's laughing and
waving to you, but he won't let me touch him."

One of the ponies threw up its head and stared; a few seconds later it kicked up its heels and both trotted away. B. burst out laughing.

"He's trying to ride the pony," she said.

A little later she turned to us. "He's gone," she said.

To our questions B. replied that Archie was dressed in a tweed jacket and grey flannel trousers, was bareheaded and appeared much amused. He had not spoken to her, but had backed away when she tried to touch him. He had appeared to be solid and three-dimensional. B. herself was normal and composed.

We joined the picnic party at the Tor, told our story, and lunched. It was a very hot day, and after some clambering on the rocks we sat in the shade of the most massive of them. There were buzzards overhead. I took out a sketch-book and began to sketch. B. lay flat on her back on my right, and was soon sound asleep. Her left hand was outstretched on the heather. After a time I noticed that the fingers of this hand were twitching and twisting. Thinking her to be awake, I spoke to her but got no answer. I bent over to look at her; she was breathing regularly and appeared to be in a deep slumber. I put my pencil between the moving fingers and it was seized and held. I then placed the sketch-book, open at a blank page, close to her hand. The hand began to write, but the writing, seen from where I sat, was both upside down and from right to left on the page. I was about to rise quietly to look at the writing from the other side of her recumbent form, when the pencil shifted to the opposite end of the page and wrote, legibly now to me but upside down and from right to left from the writer's point of view: "I forgot; of course you couldn't read it like that"—and then went on with a short message of love and reassurance, not for me, but to be passed on to the girl to whom Archie had become engaged shortly before he died. It was signed: "Archie." (I must say that I did not, after much thought about it and taking advice, pass on the message. I feared that, from so extraordinary a provenance, it was unlikely to be received as genuine, and that I should only re-open a wound.)

When B. awoke I showed her the script, and asked her to resume the same position of body and hand and to try to write upside down and from right to left. She failed completely. (Let any right-handed person who doubts this attempt it.)

There was to be one more item in the doings of this strange day. When we returned to the house in the evening one of the family, not B., remembered that she had put out that morning, and forgotten, some snap-shots to "print" by exposure to a north light. She brought us the frames with the photographs in them, all hopelessly over-exposed and dark red. But across one of the prints there appeared, in clear white capitals against the dark red background, the words MORIENS CANIS. This could be Latin for "Dying you sing" (or third-form Latin for "the dying dog"). The white of these capital letters was not superimposed upon the red, but was the white of the unexposed printing-paper. It remained unaffected by the light.

I have, as I have said, no comment to make upon the "apport" of the brooch or upon B.'s assertion, not to be doubted by anyone knowing her and still less by one watching her at the time, that she had experienced the physical sensations of hearing and seeing Archie Gordon in broad daylight. But the fact that, on seeing her fingers twitch, I at once put a pencil into her hand, is evidence to me that this affair must have taken place after B. had developed the capacity for what is called "automatic writing." For there had been an occasion, in the library of her London home, when B., who knew neither Latin nor Greek, had written, rapidly and without hesitation, passages from Livy and Xenophon, her Greek script flowing as readily, complete with accents, as her Latin. Her brother and myself were present, and when the "control," whatever it was, went on to write down numbers of the pages where the passages cited were to be found, we were disappointed to discover no trace of them when we turned to those pages in the library editions of these authors. But the control wrote: "Not there; in the little bookshelf upstairs," and in the little bookshelf upstairs we found two small school-editions of Livy and Xenophon with the passages on the pages as given to us by "the control." I should add that the "control" had begun by declaring "its" intention of giving us proof that "it" was an independent intelligence and not a part of B.'s subconscious.

What I cannot now remember—and B. is no longer living to remind me—is whether her gift for automatic writing came before or after her family's London house had been disturbed by some very violent manifestations of the kind usually attributed to a "poltergeist." I was rung up one evening, in the "digs" I shared in Bedford Court Mansions, by B.'s mother, who had just met a table from one of the bedrooms walking by itself downstairs. What did I advise? I had no advice to give. That night B.'s bed, her mother's bed, a sister's bed, were lifted off the ground and swayed about. The climax was the appearance in B.'s room of a little, old cripple, whom she recognised as the gardener who had looked after the Square when she was a child. He had hanged himself in a house in the Square many years before, but B. and the other children had not been told of this. With great courage B. told him this nonsense must stop, and then prayed for him. That was the end of the disturbances.

W. B. Yeats came to hear about B., and I was asked to be present at a meeting between the celebrated poet and the unsophisticated girl at the flat of one of B.'s friends, Mrs Fowler. Yeats looked like a gross exaggeration of the Idea of a Poet, as laid up in heaven. He was dressed in very loose, hanging black clothes; he wore an immense broad-brimmed black hat and a flowing cloak. One raven lock fell over his forehead. When the tea-cakes had been eaten, he asked B. to "write" for him. She sat with pencil and paper, and almost immediately the pencil began the most furious scribblings, so violent that it often fell from her fingers. The scribblings were at first quite illegible; later on we were able to decipher them. They consisted of violent abuse of B., with threats to harm her. "Some day I will show myself to you, and that means madness and death." Yeats at once took charge. "Leave this spirit to me," he said; "I will exorcise him." He then rose to his great height, and taking a stick—or was it the poker?—he drew a complicated pattern on the carpet ("Would you mind moving the tea-table a trifle? Thank you") while muttering incantations.

"There," he said; "that will settle him. He cannot harm you now."

B. took up her pencil and wrote: "Ha! ha! if you think that folly can stop me, you will find you are badly mistaken." The deflation of Yeats was complete. His long, angular body subsided into an arm-chair. He had the beaten look of a defeated boxer in his corner.

Victory, however, seemed to have a soothing effect on B.'s pencil. It was now willing to answer questions calmly, even civilly. The writer's name was Thomas Creech. He had been "a translator." He had been Vicar of Welwyn. He had killed himself in 1700, at Oxford. "Why?" "Some said it was money troubles, others that it was for love. They were wrong. I was afraid of being found out."

"Found out in what?"

"Cruelty—to boys."

Yeats, who might well have known the name of the first English translator of Lucretius, had no conscious memory of it; the rest of us were equally ignorant. It did not take us long to track down the facts about Thomas Creech. A. L. Smith, the Master of Balliol, took a great interest in the Oxford period of his career, and discovered a portrait of Creech. Nearly every particular given through B. then and subsequently— for Creech eventually became friendly and even penitent—was verified, except the reason for his suicide. But he had been Headmaster of Sherborne, as well as Vicar of Welwyn, and had had his opportunities.

For some years B.'s mediumistic powers, which flowered spontaneously, were of a high order; her automatic scripts were frequently "veridical" to a striking degree. It would not be too much to say that it was B. who gave to A. L. Smith and his wife, among others, an assurance that human personality can and does survive bodily death. A happy marriage to a husband who, not unnaturally, did not encourage the exercise of paranormal activities led to a gradual decrease and cessation of B.'s uncommon gifts.

An experience of a very different kind which happened to me at about this period seems worth recording, if only as a warning to others not to play about as I did, in idle mood, with the obscure and uncharted depths of the human psyche. I was on a week-end visit to a young couple, old friends of mine, at Oxford. The husband was dining in one of the colleges, and I dined alone with the wife, whom I will call Y. After dinner our talk turned to hypnotism. I had never seen a hypnotist in action, and was completely ignorant of the whole subject. But having read of "hypnotic eyes," I proposed, for fun, to attempt to hypnotise my hostess. I had no idea of how to set about it, beyond staring fixedly into my victim's eyes, at the same time "willing" her to go into a trance. Being naturally impatient, and by no means believing that anything could come of it, I feel sure my stare lasted less than sixty seconds. But it was enough. Y. did not go into a trance, or become, at first, in any way changed as far as her mental processes went, but she was struck dumb. All attempts at speech failed her; she could only make a sound like "wa-wa-wa." At first we were both amused; but when her state of aphasia continued, I began to be alarmed. Y. took pencil and paper and answered my many questions in writing. She kept her head, but naturally begged me to think of some way of undoing what I had done. I was completely at a loss. I tried all tones of voice; bracing commands to pull herself together; gentle pleading; ridicule. Y. could only say "wa-wa-wa." After a time her expression changed. She looked deeply unhappy, became very restless, and kept looking at her right foot.

"Look at my foot," she wrote; "it's a club-foot." I assured her it was nonsense and pulled her to her feet; she stumped about the room, dead-lame, and persistently pointing to her foot. Her expression was by now so far-away, so unfamiliar, so unhappy, that I had the feeling that I was alone with a stranger, a person unknown. She no longer wrote replies to my questions. She began to look at me with suspicion, her eyes now furtive and hostile. At this point—it must have been past eleven o'clock—I heard her husband returning. I went to meet him in the hall. I explained what I had done, and tried to prepare him for the extraordinary change in his young wife's personality, indeed for the disappearance of her personality. Luckily his scientific curiosity saved me, to my relief, from reproaches and himself from dismay. He gleamed with interest, almost with amusement. But when we entered the drawing-room, Y. flew at him. He seized her arm, and she tried to bite his wrist. He spoke to her gently, but there was no recognition in her eyes, which were those of a dumb, resentful animal. She was, in the old phrase, as "one possessed." Her husband remained calm, patient and undismayed. I cannot remember how long he continued to soothe and quiet her, but in the end she became somnolent, and allowed him to lead her to bed. She slept soundly, and woke next morning completely restored. She remembered the events of the night before only to the point where she had still been able to write messages for me. But all that day, as she went about her ordinary pursuits, she continued to limp.

There was a curious sequel. About a year later I again went to spend a night with this couple. I arrived to find Y. at tea with two women-visitors, strangers to me.

She stood up to shake hands with me across the tea-table, but as our eyes met, she was again struck dumb. I heard the "wa-wa-wa" beginning, as she tried to greet me. I said: "I'm sorry, but I have a most urgent message for you, which can't wait." She followed me out of the room. In the hall I said, with care not to meet her eyes, "Y. this won't do. You *must* pull yourself together." She laughed and said: "It's all right now." And it was, and has ever since remained, all right.

But I have never again looked long, however great the temptation, into a woman's eyes. I should add that both husband and wife have read and confirmed this account of these odd happenings.

## CHAPTER V

# "GOING DOWN, SIR!"

FOR those among us who fail to achieve distinction at large, it is nice to be assured that we belong at any rate to one small, exclusive class. I have a feeling that the number of civilians who had, before the year 1910, successfully fired a practice-torpedo from a submerged submarine into a British cruiser, eliciting the flag signal: "Well done," cannot be great. Yet I am one of that number.

Not that the feat in itself was a difficult one. All the necessary calculations had already been made by the submarine's commander, and all I had to do was to hold a pistol in my right hand, look into some sort of reflector where I saw a small cruiser crossing from right to left, and squeeze the trigger at the moment that the cruiser passed a cross scratched on the centre of the reflector. The trigger released a torpedo with a dummy head; and in due course the cruiser made the congratulatory signal to record a hit.

No, it was not the hitting of the target that was unusual, but that I, a young man reading for the Bar, should have been several fathoms under the surface of St Andrew's Bay in one of His Majesty's submarines during a naval exercise. It all came of my having a sailor-brother. He commanded a submarine; the submarine was at Dundee; I was on a shooting-visit in the neighbourhood, and he invited me to spend a couple of days and a night as a guest in his ship. That it was strictly forbidden for civilians to be taken on cruises did not seem to matter, since I was given one of his spare caps to wear on my head, a tarpaulin jacket, an enormous muffler that all but hid my face, a pair of sea-boots and a sweater. In this disguise, and crouching low in the dinghy, I was rowed out to the submarine without catching any eyes that mattered.

The submarine belonged to the A class. Except for its periscope and conning-tower, it had little in common with a modern submarine. Its shape was more like that of a Rugby football than a cigar. The interior of the hull, apart from the torpedo-tubes and the tanks into and from which water was alternately taken in and blown out to cause the boat to submerge or to surface, was one single chamber, crowded with machinery. Between the machines two officers and the crew lived, worked, ate and slept. Everything inside the hull could be seen from everywhere else, but nothing outside could be seen except by one man's eye, at the eye-piece of the periscope.

As a place to live and sleep in, even for thirty-six hours, an A-class submarine lacked all amenities. (As a landsman I should have said necessaries, since when I asked my brother: "Where do we ——?" he said: "We don't at sea.") My sleeping place was a thin mattress stretched beneath some engine which ran all night to keep the hull lit and ventilated. There was about nine inches of clearance between my face and the complicated, involuted coils of this humming machine. Fortunately I do not suffer from claustrophobia. But the Royal Navy always makes the best of things, and

4

our dinner was a superb chicken *en casserole*, cooked and served in an old biscuit-tin.

These early submarines did not make prolonged journeys under water in peacetime. We may have been submerged for an hour during the exercise with the cruiser, but otherwise our practice consisted mainly of short spells of submerging to various depths and re-surfacing. When the hull, by taking in water-ballast, had reached the required depths, it was necessary to maintain that depth while travelling by working some arrangement of planes or rudders. This was done by a large wheel, at which I was expected to take my turn, stripped to the waist. A clock-hand on a dial showed the depth to be maintained, and it took some practice before the ship could be held steady. I remember causing some amusement among the crew as we rose and fell and undulated under my wheelmanship. I also recall my pride when I got the knack, and the pointer kept comparatively still. There were a few moments during a practice-dive which are still vivid to me. My brother had decided to submerge to something like the permissible limit for those days, and stood at his command-post under the conning-tower calling out various orders; at the same time a Petty Officer (was he the Bosun?) who stood watching a depth-gauge called out the figures on the gauge, adding: "Going down, sir," or: "Coming up, sir," as the case might be. This Petty Officer had a ringing and most expressive voice, quite unlike the flat duty-voice characteristic of the services. Whether he really had any cause for anxiety I have no idea, but when he called out figures in the sixties the changing inflexions of his voice were decidedly disquieting to one who had never been under the sea before.

"Sixty-six going down, sir."

"Sixty-seven going *down*, sir."

"Sixty-nine going DOWN, sir."

There really did seem to me to be a note of urgency, even of complaint, as the word 'down' was pronounced with increasing emphasis, on an ascending scale. Thoughts have the speed of light, almost; and I had time to remember the not so few accidents to A-boats in the last few years, and to imagine the feelings of my parents if two sons of theirs, and one of them where he had no business to be, were to perish together on the floor of St Andrew's Bay. Meanwhile my brother was giving out orders in a perfectly unconcerned way; orders to blow No. 3 tank, to blow No. 4 tank, and long before my rapid meditations had reached a joint memorial service—there could be no funeral, since the sands would so soon engulf our machine-cluttered tomb—the Bosun's voice had changed.

"Seventy-three coming UP! sir."

I could see the gauge myself: seventy-two—seventy—sixty-eight—decidedly we were coming up. I felt very cheerful and experienced and seaman-like. If my brother had shared even a fraction of the Petty Officer's relief when the downward movement ended and the upward movement began, he showed no sign of it. I am inclined to think now that the whole fleeting drama in my mind was due not to any approach to danger on the submarine's descent towards the sea-bed, but to the fact that the Petty Officer was a born actor with the imagination of a Walter Mitty. He was probably just enjoying himself.

I must draw a veil over my only other adventure on

that brief trip. It was all very well for professional submariners to say "We don't," but I was a land-lubber. The rope, the contraption, the slippery curving turtle-back, the shameful publicity—how I wished that I could have drawn that veil then.

## CHAPTER IV

# BEHIND THE LINES

DURING the eight years that ended with the outbreak of war in 1914, propaganda in high places had completely succeeded in "selling," as the Americans would say, the French to the British. The Entente Cordiale was more than a policy between governments; it was an acceptable and accepted attitude of mind between peoples. If we still called our allies "the frogs" when we disembarked our horses on the quay at Boulogne, it was a term of affection; and if the very first letters home which came before me to be censored, written from a windy rest-camp among the dunes of the Pas de Calais, said "This place is not a patch on Blighty," the criticism was of the bleak discomforts of a camp and not of the French. From the sentry on the quay who responded to a discreet enquiry with a wide and hospitable sweep of the arm and "N'importe où, mon Lieutenant, içi c'est la France," to the girls in the estaminet, all was friendliness and welcome.

There were language difficulties, of course. The yeoman who, wishing to buy eggs, and finding that "oofs" meant nothing to the farmer's wife, bent down and touched his horse's hooves, failed to make his meaning clearer. And the Old Etonian (I blush to write it) who, having seen "Défense d'afficher" on a wall, asked a Frenchman where it was possible to afficher, did not get much further in his quest. But such misunderstandings were more amusing than irritating, and once the British soldier had won recognition for his celebrated "Na poo" language, means of communication were serviceable enough for troops on their way through France to that British enclave (for which the French Government were said, alas, to have put in a claim for rent), the front-line trenches.

But when it came to settling down, for long periods of training or "rest," in the French villages and farms, things were different. It has long been my conviction that if you want nations to love one another, you must keep them apart. I can only go with the "get-together" school of thought in so far as getting together is confined to those who, by education, curiosity or the gift of sympathetic imagination, can easily and happily put themselves into a foreigner's shoes. Such people are not rare; there are probably more of them in Great Britain than in any other country in the world; they embrace, I suppose, a majority of those who used to be known, with no serious imprecision, as gentlefolk. These people, with a smattering of foreign history and literature, a delight in variety, an eye for character and a capacity for doing without tea and marmalade, have always been able to make friends with, and see the point of, foreigners. But the minds of the bulk of the British troops in the first Great War—perhaps even in the second—were not so elastic. In our very first billets, at Wormhout in Flanders, my machine-gunners began to complain. They did not like being asked to pay for the use of a bicycle-pump when their football needed to be blown up. My sergeant, himself a farmer, was profoundly shaken at discovering that a twelve-year-old girl

managed the bull and his business, albeit with as grave a
face as her charge. These reactions, to miserliness and to
matter-of-factness about reproduction, both reminded
me that in England we have no peasants; our farmers
belong to a class that has acquired "nice" minds, and
our labourers reflect, for the most part, the minds of their
employers. To myself, and to my brother-officers, the
French peasant was known through literature, talk or
travel; we expected to find in these small owners or
crop-sharers the earthiness and frugality of the authentic
European peasant, and we did find it. To myself the
great oblong, bricked-in basin, six foot deep in semi-
liquid manure, around which stood the farm-buildings
with the dwelling-house itself, was a reminder of A. L.
Smith's lectures on Maitland and the key-position of the
muck-heap in our early social history. But to my men
it was just a stinking affront. (All the more credit to
one of our Yeomen who, when his horse, on being led
out shining for a General's inspection, backed into this
filth and was totally submerged, refrained from all but
these moving and heartfelt words: "Oh, that I 'ad the
wings of a dove, for then would I floy away, floy away
and be at rest!")

Then, again, we officers had better teeth than our
men. Before an army can fight on its stomach, its
rations must pass the barrier of teeth, and in 1914, when
there was no health service, this was just what the hard
ration-biscuit too often failed to do. Soaked biscuit is
wretched fare; and on pay-day the men flocked to the
bakers' shops, and were disgusted to find, instead of
square white British loaves with thin, flexible sides,
those long crusty "flutes," delectable if you are a com-
missioned officer and can bite, but sadly disappointing

to a rank-and-file capable only of chewing. "Bread is the staff of life," complained some wag in those days, "but the life of the Staff is one long loaf," and the long loaves in the bakeries were no less a grievance. Another bad mark for our brave allies.

Accordingly, when the Battle of Loos, behind which we had stood saddled-up all night in the rain, hoping to push through a "gap" at dawn, petered out in stalemate, and the cavalry divisions were dispersed throughout the countryside far from the sound of the guns, our men were already disillusioned and disapproving. Nor was it all narrow-mindedness. Their dislike of seeing women and girls doing the heavy labour of field and farm was rooted in genuine chivalry. The cupidity of the French peasant over trifles, unworthy even of the very poor, revolted them. And they were never admitted, as were their officers, to the inner chambers of those dishevelled farmhouses. They entered the kitchen, where the hens croaked and clucked about the unswept floor, but never the Sunday parlour or the best bedroom. In there, commandeered as officers' billets, all was cleanliness and order. The marriage-wreath lay beneath a bell-glass on the chimney-piece. The brick floor was scrubbed; the heavy presses shone with polish; the white counterpanes were spotless. And, although the billeting-money was good, the welcome of the farmer's wife seldom appeared to be wholly mercenary. Could our N.C.O.'s and men have spoken French, they might have been surprised at the level of the peasant's conversation. They would have learnt of the pinch of conscription, of the drag of the implacable land upon the energies of women and old men. They would have seen their enemies not as tiresome "Jerries" but as detestable "*sales Boches.*" They would have heard that the British alliance was understood and valued, and heard it in graceful and rounded phrases that could be matched in few English farmyards.

And when our Yeomanry settled down for the middle months of the winter at D., a pleasant country town in the neighbourhood of Boulogne, we officers, at least, were offered real hospitality. It took us a day or two to fall into the habit of hand-shaking at every encounter, however casual, however frequent, with the well-to-do inhabitants in whose houses we were billeted. My own bedroom and machine-gun H.Q. were in the house of a manufacturing shoemaker, a kindly, bearded man with whom I shook hands eight times between breakfast and lunch on the first morning. For his office and mine were in the same passage; we had to pass and repass, and a formal handshake was *de rigueur* on each occasion. I learnt to dodge this by watchfulness and listening for footsteps or for the creak of an opening door, and was able, by practice, to reduce the daily shakes to a manageable number. But, during the months I spent there, I never got on nodding terms with my good host. To the last it was a question of evade or shake.

This master-shoemaker, who ran a large factory, was a keen shot. He and the Mayor, the Juge de Paix, the chemist and other notables of D., ran a shooting syndicate, and were kind enough on several occasions to invite my brother-officers and myself to shoot with them. The shoots, which always took place on a Sunday, were very formal affairs. They began with an immense luncheon at noon in one of the inns on the *place*, a spacious cobbled square. There were many courses, four or five different kinds of admirable wines, the drinking of healths, compliments and jokes, and it was at earliest two o'clock of the short winter day before the coffee and liqueurs had been lingered over, and we crowded, rosy and talkative, into cars to drive to the forest. The forest was immense, with broad rides dividing it into a series of rectangles. It held a few pheasants, referred to as "*le fruit défendu*," for there was a ban on killing them; but we were out for woodcock and rabbits, and there were plenty of both.

There was an obstinate tradition in England, especially fostered by *Punch*, that a Frenchman out shooting is a figure of fun. His clothes are absurd; his aim is wild and dangerous; he prefers sitting targets; he makes no distinction between game-birds and song-birds. A shopkeeper out shooting, as the "Mr Briggs" series testified, was equally a cause for ridicule and alarm in the eyes of true sportsmen. I must confess that when I found myself for the first time standing in a ride between two French shopkeepers, I felt a trifle uneasy. There had been a universal drawing-on of wide waterproof trousers when we got out of the cars which, done with a certain ritual solemnity, had faintly reminded me of the "comic" tradition. But it was my experience of woodcock that caused my unease. That silent bird, appearing from nowhere at or even below the level of a man's head, and full of jinks and changes of direction, thinks nothing of flying down a line of guns. If *Punch* had been only partially right about Mr Briggs and "Mossoo," might it not be a case for falling flat on my face at the first appearance of so wayward and wavering a target? I need not have worried. The Juge de Paix and his colleagues were as reliable as could be. They knew, and kept to, all the rules of safe shooting. Without brilliance, they were steady, reliable shots. My personal pre-occupation was only to kill my share, and not to fall too far below expectations raised by the first shot of the day when, not having been warned, I brought down a really tall *fruit défendu* in a style that surprised myself as highly as it roused the admiration of my hosts. As for the organisation of the shoot, it was perfect. By some means known only to a nation of functionaries, the syndicate was able to dispose of a company of second-line troops as beaters. These were divided into platoons, and so distributed about the rides of the vast woodlands that, no sooner was one beat finished, than, at the sound of a horn, another beat was begun. There were keepers and dogs for the pick-up; no shouting or gesticulating, but a quiet intentness on the business in hand. One afternoon, a wild-boar having been reported by the *garde-champêtre*, we were given slugs to load into the left barrels of our twelve-bores. He did not appear, but on a later Sunday when I was on leave, he did break cover, and was shot dead by our Brigade padre, Humphrey Barclay. I wish I had been there, for the "*hallali*" was sounded over the dead boar, and no end of ceremonies and toasts took place in celebration. The only blot on these enjoyable expeditions was the short-ness of their duration. By four o'clock it was twilight, and we had to knock off. But before returning to D., the whole party repaired to a pitch-pine room in a chalet-restaurant, to gather round a log-fire and drink sweet and sticky liqueurs, with more jokes and compli-ments. It was all great fun, as well as giving us a vivid glimpse at Frenchmen practising their celebrated art of living.

Nor do I forget the tea-parties, with Earl Grey tea

in delicate shallow cups, with my host's two married nieces. These gay and prosperous grass-widows, whose husbands were serving in the army, were young and pretty and as fond of "officers" as any Lydia Bennet. They had the fair hair and blue eyes so admired by Frenchmen, spoke good English, and made no bones about their enjoyment of being semi-detached. The rules for married women must have been strict indeed at D., for: "What *would* my husband say!" was a constant and gleeful comment upon any casual and fleeting *tête-à-tête*, in street or shop, between themselves and ourselves. As a rule they entertained together, but I recollect an occasion when the prettier of the pair, at a chance morning encounter, invited me into her own home, an agreeable eighteenth-century house that faced upon the *place*. I was somewhat surprised, after a glass of liqueur in the pretty drawing-room, to be pressed to go upstairs to inspect the conjugal bedroom, and then to tell her what her husband would say to that? Luckily she quickly replied to herself that he would have a fit, and when I had admired the bedspread and the view from the windows, we went downstairs again and I took my leave.

These two frank and friendly young women entertained the younger officers of the whole Brigade and enlivened our masculine routine. Whether their husbands would in fact have had anything to say worth saying, I have no idea. Nor can I be sure that either of them had any link with a mysterious incident which caused me to be a good deal chaffed. At the end of the first day's march on our departure from D., there appeared upon the linoleum-covered table in a kitchen where we sat down to dine a large, neatly packed brown-paper parcel addressed to myself. How it got there I was never able to discover, but I was incautious enough to open it in the presence of my brother-officers. It contained one of those expensive flat linen hats, with broad edges of elaborate lace, worn by very young boy-babies in those faraway days. And attached to the hat was a card, inscribed in a thin, slanting, feminine hand:

"*De la part de quelqu'une qui vous trouve très bien mais très timide.*"

That, among the rude and licentious soldiery, took a good deal of living down.

Three years later, in two German prison-camps, I again found the company of French officers wholly congenial, and I returned from the war strengthened in my liking and respect for our so intelligent, articulate, and civilised allies. But there is no blinking the truth that several million Englishmen came home from France with hearts in which the Entente Cordiale was dead. Two nations had "got to know each other better"— —that nostrum of Anglo-this and Anglo-that societies —and had liked each other less. Alliances can be, alas, as tragically disruptive as war itself.

## CHAPTER VII

# PROMOTION FOR THE

# DOCTOR

IT was only after making sure that the M.O. was well
on his way to the Officers' Mess for dinner that two
of my brother-officers tied an apple to the handle of
the anteroom door. For it was important that he should
be the first to find it there, and to ask as he entered,
pendant cheeks quivering, what the deuce the apple was
for? The answer came in chorus: "An apple a day keeps
the doctor away." Always the good fellow among us,
he took the joke easily enough, but the chaff was
intended less lightly than its victim liked to pretend.
There was already, in these early days before the regiment embarked for France, a feeling among us that, if
it came to going sick, it was decidedly better to be an
officer than a private soldier.

It must be admitted that the health of the regiment,
statistically, was first-class. If "Medicine and Duty" is
to be the certain result of parading sick, no matter what
you are suffering from, there is not much point in
parading, especially when the medicine is all but
invariably Number Nine. It is the duty of every
regimental M.O. to have a short way with malingerers,
but among volunteer soldiers in wartime, malingering
is rare indeed. It was this that our doctor never under-

stood; he believed it to be due to his gruff, suspicious and bullying way with the sick that his parade-states were so often blank, and he took open pride in it. No doubt his manner did keep men from going sick; but it is the genuine, not the fraudulent, sufferer who most resents a public accusation of "swinging the lead."

It was not until we had been six months in France that an incident in which I was personally involved revealed the eccentricity of our M.O.'s views about his responsibilities. It was winter, and the regiment was billeted in one of those straggling villages of Northern France where small houses of red and white bricks alternate with dilapidated barns and outhouses of plastered rubble and timbers. I was roused from my bed some time after midnight by an improperly dressed corporal, who reported that one of my machine-gun team had met with an accident and "seemed very bad." Dressed only a degree less sketchily than the corporal, I hurried down the deserted street, ramshackle under the moving yellow blob from my torch, to the barn where the injured man was lying. To reach him I had to climb a ladder to a hay-loft, where he and others had spread their blankets in the hay; a group of bent or kneeling figures surrounded the victim, and a good deal of loud talk and argument was going on. The man himself was writhing in pain; his hair was damp and matted, and sweat was streaming down his contorted features. I recognised him as one of the drivers, a rather tough customer, recently posted to the section, who had been giving a good deal of trouble. There was no mystery about his injury: one of his knees was dislocated; his leg below the knee stuck out at an unnatural angle. Except that he had been "playing the fool" I never discovered what had caused the dislocation, but it was clearly a simple case of putting the knee back into place. Since several of his fellows had already tried to do this, causing the man to yell but with no effect on the knee, I went up the street again to fetch the doctor.

The doctor was not pleased at being woken. He was a Major, and I was a Lieutenant, and he wanted to know by whose authority I had disturbed the rest of my superior officer. I told him I had a man with his knee out, and in pain.

"Then let him parade sick tomorrow morning."

"But he can't move——"

"I'll see him in his billet in the morning."

"But I tell you, he's in great pain."

"He would be, with a dislocated knee."

"You will get up and come now. You can't leave a man in pain all night."

"That's not the way to speak to me, Jones."

"Are you coming?"

"I have told you. In the morning."

"Then I shall go and fetch the Colonel."

At that the doctor got up, grumbling, dressed and came with me to the barn. There being little room in the hay-loft, I remained at the foot of the ladder while the doctor climbed it to examine his patient.

In no time he was down again. All the cloudy vexation had passed from his puffy grey face. His eyes were genial and friendly, with a conspiratorial gleam in them. He put his hand under my elbow and pushed me towards the door of the barn.

"Come outside a moment, Jones. I've had a brainwave."

We went into the darkness and stood by the manure-heap.

"Isn't this the man you had all that trouble with?"

"Yes."

"I thought so. Well now, here's a chance for you. If I leave that knee out till tomorrow, it will be in such a state that you'll have to send him down to base. It will be months, I should say, before he'll walk again. It's more than likely that you'll be rid of him for good."

"You mean, leave him in pain deliberately?"

"It won't kill him."

"And you call yourself a doctor?"

"I'm only trying to do you a good turn."

"Do you really want me to get the Colonel out of bed?"

The doctor, on reflection, did not. Muttering something about how hard it was to help people, and the folly of missing such a chance, he climbed the ladder again and pulled the groaning rapscallion's knee into place.

Next morning, still boiling, I told the story to my Colonel. Sidney Peel, who never minced matters, informed the authorities that, so far as his regiment was concerned, the doctor must go. And go he did. But the R.A.M.C. now found themselves with an officer on their hands whom nobody wanted. With a gesture reminiscent of the Crimean War and the honours given to Dr Andrew Smith, they promoted our doctor to the rank of Colonel and put him in charge of a large base hospital. Of how the patients in that hospital fared, no rumour ever reached us. Promotion is sweet; let us hope that it sweetened that sour heart.

## CHAPTER VIII

# A MOST ENJOYABLE EVENING

SQUADRON-QUARTERMASTER-SERGEANT WHITE came to France in the third autumn of the First World War as a replacement. He was an excellent quartermaster, one of that not too common type who held that the stores entrusted to their care were intended, not to be hoarded and amassed, but to be given out to the troops. He was good-tempered and industrious, and popular with us all. But there was something persistently civilian about him; his rather tubby figure, his plump white hands, his soft voice, belonged, you felt, to a shop not to a camp, and, even when he wore his soldier's cap, a pencil was apt to get lodged behind his ear. I was, accordingly, mildly surprised when, having ridden down from the front line to make some arrangements for supplies, I was approached by Q.M.S. White and asked whether I could do him a favour. He had now, he explained in his quiet tradesman's voice, been several months in France and had never seen the trenches or the front line. It did not look well in his letters home. After all, there was a war on, but he so far had seen nothing of it. Could I give him permission to go up to the front line with the rations one of these evenings, and have a look round? Q.M.S. White was a key man, and not to be lightly regarded as expendable. I have not the slightest doubt that I ought to have said No. But my machine-gunners were in a very quiet sector of the trenches near Laventie, on loan to "the Bantams," and I had not the heart to refuse him.

The rations were brought up when darkness fell, and I was in the Headquarters dugout when Sergeant White reported to me. He looked very spick and span in his clean uniform and shining buttons, which contrasted oddly with the black or yellow tarpaulin jackets and sou'westers worn by the rest of us, for it was autumn and the trenches were low-lying and oozed mud and slime. In the light of the candles stuck in bottles, which illuminated my cavern, Q.M.S. White's bright buttons and correct service dress seemed to enhance his customary look of a non-combatant among fighting men. But his eyes were even brighter than his buttons; had he been a dog, Q.M.S. White would have been wagging his tail.

I handed him over to one of the N.C.O.s to make a tour of the front-line trench and visit the machine-gun positions. And in no time I forgot Q.M.S. White, for a message came through from the Infantry to say that a patrol was to go out into no-man's-land at such and such an hour and place, and I was kept busy with detailed orders to my machine-gunners. I forget what the patrol was to do, but it was unsuccessful. There was a sudden spurt of Verey lights from the German front trench; hostile mortars came into action and machine-guns began to rattle. One member of the patrol was killed, and several wounded; stretcher-bearers came panting up the communication trenches and had to crawl gingerly over the parapet, rifle-shooting began from both lines, and my machine-gunners thumped the handles of their Vickers guns as they traversed to keep the German heads down. It was a real fracas while it lasted, noisy and confused; the sky full of fireworks, the cratered waste ground between the lines white and black by turns, the close night-horizon dotted with recurrent red flashes, bullets cracking like whips. But it did not last long; our dead and wounded were retrieved, first aid was given on the firing-step, and the stretchers went swaying away down the communication trenches, the dead man's boots sticking out from the blanket that covered him like the boots of all other dead men. I returned to my dugout from a final tour of my gun-positions with that sense of dull fatigue induced by failure. It had not been my failure, but there had been waste, a life lost, some very ugly wounds, and much confusion. Nor had anything been accomplished.

I was writing a routine report of this very minor but regrettable incident when Q.M.S. White reappeared in the entrance of the dugout. He was covered with mud; his face was red and sweaty, his crumpled sleeves were turned up and his white hands and forearms so sticky with blood that he carried them stiffly away from his body, as Charles Laughton did when he played Macbeth.

"Hullo Q.M.S. White. Still here? Have you been hit?"

"Oh no, sir, only practising my First Aid. I attended a course last year, sir. I must be getting back now, sir, but I just wanted to thank you for a most enjoyable evening." He saluted, beaming, and went out.

I was seconded from my unit shortly afterwards and hardly saw Q.M.S. White again. But he must have enjoyed at least one more party, and presumably a better one still, since I learnt, at the end of the war, that S.Q.M.S. White had been killed in action.

## CHAPTER IX

# NOTHING LIKE MONEY

THERE cannot have been many occasions, since the abolition of purchase in the British Army, when an officer has been able to achieve, if not promotion, at any rate, the sort of commendation that leads to promotion by the expenditure of cash. Yet on one occasion that is just what I succeeded in doing. And although I personally paid out the cash, in wads of dirty French francs, across a table, it was not even my own money.

Put like that, it sounds fishy enough, but at the time I had quite other thoughts in my head. What I imagined myself to be paying for was shock treatment for a bad case of apathy and discouragement. In January 1918, during the lull on the British front while the Germans were preparing for their great onslaught in March, I was appointed to command the Divisional Machine-Gun Company of the 19th Infantry Division. How the 19th Division acquired this unfortunate unit, or what its previous history had been, I cannot remember, although General "Ma" Jeffreys must have explained it to me when I was welcomed by him in person on arrival at his H.Q. and invited to dinner. What I do remember was his warning that I had a tough job, and his promise that I could look to his staff, and even to himself, for support.

It was midwinter, but I found my company bivouacking in a wood. There was a small wooden hut in which the company commander had his office and slept; the other officers and men were living under groundsheets stretched over branches or stakes, the mules stabled in tumbledown farm-sheds. There was a steady drip from the trees; the men were huddling in waterproof capes and, sure sign of demoralisation among the N.C.O.'s, there were matted locks hanging out beneath the men's hats, and even reports of men parading unshaven.

It was clear at a glance that this was no case for "strafing" or kicking up a row. Authority, not themselves, had neglected these men to the point of forfeiting its right to make demands upon them. For they were not in the line; they were resting: and there had been no enemy pressure, no unforeseen mishap to supplies, to excuse those responsible for their plight. I spent the next few days on horseback, visiting the various divisional, and even corps, branches of supply. The results, to one accustomed to the grudging, snubbing, triplicate-minded attitude of certain Cavalry D.A.Q.-M.G.'s, were miraculous. In three days all the men were housed in new, watertight, well-warmed Nissen huts. They were reclothed. Supplies of all sorts for men, mules and guns were delivered to us not only in sufficiency but speedily. At the end of a week my company had no more excuses for being slovenly, and no more excuses were accepted. By the exertions and efficiency of the Divisional "Q", the right to command had been restored to me.

Before, however, we had settled down, the new machine-gun battalions had been formed, and my company, no longer an independent unit under

Divisional H.Q., became one of four companies under the command of Lieut.-Colonel (later Brigadier-General) Peter Winser. This formidable figure, of height, bulk and features that precisely expressed his strong authoritative personality, was a leader after my own heart. In peace no soldier, but a great polo-player, horseman and hunting man, he was now the most single-minded warrior imaginable. Ruthless in his dealings with slackness and incompetence, he could be kindly, and indeed most charming, towards those whom he suspected of sharing his loathing for the war and determination to win it. That a German attack was imminent was known to us, and Winser's preparations for meeting it were thorough. Never before or since have I worked such long hours, or enjoyed so few moments of leisure, as during those six weeks before the German assault. And yet even now I look back on that period as the most exhilarating, the most inwardly rewarding, of my life. In the event, all our work went for nothing. Our numerous elaborate systems of defence in depth, with alternatives to meet this or that contingency, were not, on the day, even manned by ourselves. And a dense fog, in which machine-gunners were helpless, enabled the Germans to walk through our "impregnable" gun-positions almost without loss. But that was later; the cash transaction I set out to record took place soon after we joined the battalion. The other three companies had been well-found and disciplined at the time when they came under Peter Winser's orders, but, knowing the British soldier's love of competition, the Colonel decided to use this affection for putting a still brighter polish upon the appearance of his troops. Accordingly he offered a trophy—a silver hunting-horn

—to be competed for by the companies, and to be awarded monthly for the smartest turn-out of men, mules and limbers. But C Company, my own, was still far behind the others, especially as regards the mules and harness, and, unwilling to see us publicly disgraced, the Colonel kindly suggested that we should stand down on this occasion and compete a month later. But I had no mind to allow a company, already all too conscious of its inferiority, to be further depressed, and insisted on competing. The parade was to be held the following morning, when a senior officer from another unit was to inspect us and to act as judge.

It was then that I thought of cash. Our only chance of avoiding the wooden spoon, and a public display of squalor, would be to sit up all night working upon the mules and the harness. The men had spent a long day training, and were entitled to their rest. I could not order them to forgo their sleep. Their sense of the hopelessness of competing with the other companies, whose shining harness had already shamed them, would have defeated, I felt sure, an appeal to their pride, of which they had little left. I decided to try bribery. At that time most units at the front ran their own canteen, selling at a handsome profit cigarettes bought at nominal prices from, or even freely given by, the great tobacco companies. These profits were used for buying extra food and comforts for the men, but never distributed in cash. There was an amount in hand which would, if so distributed, give a worthwhile sum to every man in the company. I consulted the senior N.C.O.'s and the canteen committee, who approved the plan. I next paraded the men and explained the position. The lure of money in hand is powerful; they all but cheered.

(That it was their own money seems never to have occurred to them.) Our mules were stabled in long sheds with open sides. All available hurricane-lamps were borrowed and hung from rafters and posts; bits, curbs, stirrups and chains, heavily rusted, were thrown into sandbags which were swung for hours, one man relieving the next; there was docking and pulling of tails, trimming of manes, clipping and curry-combing, the smell of oil and saddle-soap was pervasive. Officers worked with the men; the cookhouse was busy over broth. There was something grotesque and unmilitary about all this nocturnal bustle, lantern-lit, about and between the lines of fidgetting mules—a flurry of untimely exertions made neither for pride nor duty nor king nor country, but for money.

After the sandbags had been emptied of silvery chains, and the collars, bridles and traces hung up, soft and flexible, there were still the men's own badges and buttons to be cleaned. The nights are long in early February, and we no doubt had a couple of hours' sleep before reveille, though memory has chalked up an all-night session.

The judging next morning was a lengthy affair. The visiting officer was a most conscientious man; he lifted the feet of the mules, one after the other, to examine their frogs; he ran his hands under elbows and stifles for signs of scruffiness; he peered under collars; and after each animal or man had been thoroughly surveyed he entered marks in a small, black, shiny notebook. He was busy for at least an hour with each company. We paraded third, I think, and already attracted surprised attention as we left the mule-lines and wound up the hill in brilliant sunshine, to be ready, in the best military tradition, at least an hour before we could possibly be wanted by the judge. For in that sunshine, on that smooth short turf, we gleamed: there was no doubt about that. I thought I detected a smaller, but indubitable, gleam in Peter Winser's eye.

When the marks had been added up, checked and re-checked, C Company was declared to be the winner of the trophy by a handsome margin.

On the face of it, this incident is one which many people will think I should have tried to forget, not to record. It can easily be argued that it is a striking example of the false values and low standards of the Army in the First World War. What was Peter Winser about, offering a prize for mere "spit-and-polish" (or, as it is nowadays called, "bull"), with a great and desperate battle known to be imminent? And, even granted that a good turn-out improves morale, what pride or profit can there be in smartness achieved through bribery? Worst of all, what is to be said of a company commander who takes advantage of the soldier's simple-mindedness to bribe him with his own canteen funds?

The question about spit-and-polish could be put only by those who have had no experience of the demoralising effect of squalor, and how much a nice care for appearances can do to stave it off. (Women who have bought a new hat when life became too difficult for them will recognise this truth.) And the answer to the second question about bribery is that, in this instance, the smartness bought with money did in fact restore a pride that had been lost. C Company, after that one mercenary spurt, never again fell into apathy or slackness. They were pleased with their money, but far more pleased with themselves. So much so indeed, that

within a few weeks they had earned the highest marks
for any unit in the division from the divisional gas
officer—a distinction that only those who remember the
utter boredom and dreary discomforts of the gas-mask
routine in 1918 will appreciate. And as for the canteen
funds, I can think of no way of spending them which
could have brought more "comfort" to the troops. For
self-respect is not only a great comfort in itself; without
it nothing else tastes good. And if an incidental result
of C Company's new-born efficiency was the recommendation of the O.C. Company for command of a
battalion, critics can be reassured by being told that,
owing to the German onslaught, he never got it.

## CHAPTER X

# RUNNING AWAY

B RITISH SOLDIERS, still less officers, are not
supposed to run away in battle: if retreat they
must, it should be done slowly and sullenly, with
many a turn-about to fire parthian volleys at the
enemy; it must be a matter of manœuvre, not of flight.
So strong is this admirable tradition that I must, I suppose, be one of a very small number indeed who ran
away from the Germans in the First World War, and
not merely ran, but ran like a hare, twisting and
jinking as I went, shouting to my men to run faster still.

It happened like this. It was during the Great Retreat
that began on 21 March 1918. When there has been no
sleeping at nights the memory of dates becomes blurred,
but it was, I think, on the second or third afternoon. The
weather was of a kind more suited to peace than to war:
the blue skies of March and sunshine all day long, with
no breath of wind. There was a tinge of new green on
the open, rolling grasslands surrounding what was left
of Bapaume. Our right, because of the retreat of the
Fifth Army, was in the air, and orders to retire from
position to position came as no surprise, for on the
afternoon of the first day I had watched, through my
binoculars, long columns of Germans marching in fours
with arms sloped. They were snaking away to our right
rear, deliberate and unopposed, just out of range of my

machine-guns. It was an uncomfortable memory for the succeeding days and nights.

In the morning of the day I am recalling we had repelled a German attack from a rear line of trenches. One of my young officers, firing his gun in person, had killed or wounded twenty-seven Germans in a matter of seconds, at a range of about forty yards, as they attempted to cross a road. When I visited him he was sitting at his gun with their twenty-seven rifles, collected after the attack died out, heaped like spillikins beside him. Then came the expected order to retire, and we machine-gunners were strolling back in the hot sunshine, very thirsty, when an infantry officer hailed me to say that he had seen Germans "massing" behind a wood less than a mile away. The word "massing" to a machine-gunner is like the word "Rats!" to a fox-terrier, and seeing our new young Brigadier sitting under a tree with all his maps spread out, I went up, saluted, and asked permission to turn back with two guns—for which alone we had any ammunition left—and try to do some shooting into this "mass." The Brigadier thought it a good idea, so back I went with two gun-teams, passing through groups of lost infantry-men searching for their units. Among them was a burly Sergeant Major who, seeing that we were looking for, and not retiring from, the enemy, begged to be allowed to come with us. I needed another man to act as look-out on a flank, so rather foolishly lent him my revolver, since he was unarmed, and took him with me. In that undulating and open grass country we were soon out of sight of the last of our own stragglers, and it was a surprise, as we emerged from a shallow valley, to see a British officer, with the red-tabs of the Staff and several rows of medal-ribbons, standing quite alone in this deserted place, intent upon the wood behind which the Germans were supposed to be massing. The spick-and-span appearance of his uniform, Sam Browne belt and so on, glinting in the sunshine, proved that he had not been sharing our own experiences since the Germans had attacked. It is true that in retirement, when units become confused and headquarters are often hastily abandoned, Staff officers are not such rare birds as they are during the settled routine of trench warfare. But a solitary, fantastically clean one, alone and on foot well out beyond a retiring army, was definitely an unexpected sight. It struck me as stranger still that, having turned to look at us, he at once walked quickly away to a flank, and into a sunken track. You would have thought that, whatever the reason for his presence in this lonely no-man's-land, a British officer would have made contact with any group of British soldiers advancing in good order towards the enemy. I became at once anxious to speak to this Staff officer and hurried to the point where he had disappeared. I followed the sunken track, but in forty yards or so it emerged upon the plain; there seemed no place of concealment which a man on foot could possibly have reached in the available minutes; but the dapper, be-medalled figure was nowhere to be seen. I had to return to my men, but the burly Sergeant Major, who made a further search, was equally unsuccessful. There had been rumours, since the first foggy morning when our front line had been overrun, of Staff officers suddenly appearing with orders to the troops to retire when no such orders had been given; I had derided all such tales as fantastic. But since seeing this singular apparition, so shy of us, so alert to escape,

I have been far more ready to believe that there may have been Germans courageous enough to play the most foolhardy of parts.

We never reached the "massed" target we were hoping for. We were still about eight hundred yards from the wood when the Germans emerged from it in battalion strength, walking slowly in open order. We hurriedly went into action on the spot, for there was no available cover on that open plain; but after a few bursts the whole enemy line lay down, most of them, at that range, all but disappearing from view. But they could see us; the bullets cracked about us; and when the right hand of one of my two gunners was all but severed at the wrist, it was time to move. "Coo! Just look at that, sir!" was all the gunner said to me, holding up a fore-arm from which his hand dangled, held only by a narrow band of skin and sinew.

By moving about three hundred yards to the right we could reach another shallow sunken track leading to a slight hollow in which was a patch of dead bracken and some birch-trees. To all appearances some cover, at least from view, might be found there; cover from which to fire off our remaining belts and then retire unseen. So, having bandaged the gunner and sent him to the rear, we picked up our guns, tripods and ammunition-boxes and plodded off—plodded, because there was an annoying patch of ploughed land to be crossed. We were still in full view of the Germans, who had turned a machine-gun on to us, but, considering the range, their shooting was wretched. Everything cracked over our heads and not a man was hit.

Having reached our hollow we found conditions excellent. There was cover from view among the bracken; there was a clear field of fire to the line of Germans, lying prone, and, best of all, there was immediately behind us a sunken road winding away towards our rear—the perfect get-away. Having sent the Sergeant Major with my revolver to act as right flank-guard, I decided to take the wounded gunner's place and to fire one of the guns myself. We had only a couple of belts left and I ordered fire to be held until the range made it unlikely that we should miss.

The results were most disappointing, as far as I could see without my binoculars, which had been lost. When the Germans, who were advancing with extreme deliberation and caution after their expensive repulse a few hours earlier, were about five hundred yards away, we opened fire. They all fell down like one man, disappearing from view in the herbage. Our two guns might, or might not, have killed two of them. Impossible to say. After an interval a half-section rose, we fired; down they all went. They were obviously unable, in that bright, shimmering atmosphere, to see our gun-flashes, and there was no reply that fell anywhere near us. And so it went on; a group of grey figures rising; a burst from our guns; all the figures falling flat. After our hopes of a dense mass into which to pour bullets, a belt at a time, this was a most unrewarding game, but at least we were affording the stragglers a mile or more behind us a breathing-space for re-forming.

When our last bullets had been fired we began, in rather leisurely fashion, to take the guns from the tripods and to pack up our gear. I was busy with my own gun when I heard a jingling and rattling to our left. I looked up to see a body of Germans, not less than twenty, marching straight at us round a lone grassy spur. They were not more than forty yards or so away. Having only the guest Sergeant Major available as flank-guard, I had sent him, as bad luck would have it, to the wrong flank. We were completely surprised, and entirely unarmed. I had not even my revolver. Only our legs could save us now.

I managed to heave one gun over my shoulder while I shouted, "Leave everything—follow me" (the other gun, which had refused to part with its tripod, was abandoned.) We dashed into the sunken road and in a few yards had turned a corner. The Germans must also have been surprised, as so far no shot had been fired. Fifty yards further on, the sunken road, leading so promisingly towards our rear, curved back again and became an open track across the plain. What had appeared to be our one chance was now gone. However, we scrambled somehow up the steep bank on our right, and saw a dip, a substantial hollow, about a hundred and fifty yards ahead of us. The going was excellent, over short firm turf and slightly downhill. At fifty yards I could not resist turning my head. Five or six Germans were standing on the top of the bank up which we had scrambled, and were taking aim at us. I could only shout "zigzag" before the shooting began. Being a large man, with a Vickers-gun over my shoulder, and an officer, I was naturally the principal target. But my jinking must have been either very good or very lucky. The bullets were zipping into the turf all round me. The big Sergeant Major, who had rejoined us on the sunken road, went over like a shot rabbit, a yard from my left side. Two more of our party of five went down on my right. We had no time to see whether they were killed or only winged. We

6

just ran, and with a last gasping effort reached the hollow, collapsed at the bottom of it, completely winded.

Our immediate reaction was surprising. The three of us, simultaneously, fell into a *fou rire*. We rolled about, laughing till we cried. It cannot have been from relief, since the Germans were only a hundred and fifty yards away, and we were, for the time being, completely incapable of any more running. Further escape did not seem possible. I think we laughed primarily because the scene had been so funny. Our own surprise, the Germans' surprise; brave Englishmen running like hares from an enemy; the zigzagging; the "rabbit-shooting" aspect of it all; our collapse on the warm turf; the incongruity of our plight with the brilliance of the day, with the sudden silence and the solitude. But there is, besides, the known fact that tragedy has often one finger on comedy's trigger. The smallest mishap can raise laughter, or at any rate the inclination towards it, at a funeral.

Having pulled ourselves together, and let the hot water run out of the barrel-casing of the Vickers-gun to lighten the load, we again humped gun and tripod and started down the shallow valley which led from our sheltering hollow in the direction of Bapaume and the British Third Army. It seemed, for the first five minutes, impossible that our pursuers should not appear on the lip of the hollow. But they never did. No doubt they were suspicious of this rolling country with its low but nonetheless blind undulations: we may have been, to them, a mere interruption of some rigid Teutonic reconnaissance. As to our wounded, there was nothing to be done. Our first duty was not to be captured.

After trudging a mile or so we again encountered the Brigadier, sitting with his maps under a tree. "Hullo," he said, "I never expected to see *you* again." He told me where to find my company, and showed us a green chalk-line on the map, to which we were to retire. Nightfall, in open warfare, is a comfortless affair. A line drawn on a map by the Staff has no amenities. We had neither food nor water nor greatcoats, nor blankets. Our supper that night was one green jujube apiece to suck, from a little tin box produced from the pocket of a public-spirited private soldier. Three days later I encountered another German. This time we were face to face; the range was twenty-five yards; I was still unarmed, and he did not miss.

## CHAPTER XI

# A DRAMA IN SOHO

IT was in a prisoner-of-war camp in the centre of Karlsruhe that I came across an old friend, S. R. C. Plimsoll. A spectacled light-weight—physically, I mean—he had coxed the Balliol Torpid to the Headship of the River, and later the Balliol Eight. He was at that time a rather shy, reticent man, very self-possessed and, as a good coxswain should be, firm with his crew. I had coached the Torpid and rowed in front of his glinting, observant glasses in the Eight, and although, from his being two years my junior, we had not been intimate at Oxford, I was delighted to fall in with him at Karlsruhe, although dismayed to find him sadly crippled by his wounds. We had many talks together.

It is significant of the change that has taken place, since the placid days before the First World War, in the kind of incidents that we find startling, that I should have been sufficiently impressed by a tale of Plimsoll's to remember it, nearly forty years later, in every detail. The story he told me was this.

On an evening in the summer of 1914 Plimsoll had invited a friend to dine with him in a restaurant near Piccadilly Circus. The friend did not turn up and Plimsoll dined alone, drinking, as he was careful to tell me, half a bottle, but no more, of Burgundy. Having finished his dinner, he strolled in the warm summer air towards Soho, and soon found himself in a street crowded with market-stalls. In a mood to loiter, he was threading his way slowly from stall to stall when he heard the sound of a violin. Plimsoll was a music-lover and a frequenter of concerts, and he recognised at once that he was hearing fiddle-playing of a very high order indeed. "There were not," he told me, "more than two or three fiddlers in London that season capable of such superb execution." Excited and curious, he followed the sound, and soon discovered that its source must be at the end of a narrow, dark passage which struck into the houses at right angles to the market-street. And it was here, he explained, that the half-bottle of Burgundy came in. For Plimsoll was not, he confessed, by nature adventurous or "cheeky"; without the Burgundy he would never have tried the handle of a closed door, as he tried it now. This door was at the further end of the short passage; a ray of light showed beneath it, and to anyone standing in the passage there could be no question but that the master-fiddler was playing on the other side of it.

So Plimsoll turned the handle and pushed the door open. He found himself looking into a small, square well, open to the sky. The walls were bare and grimy, but the floor, which was brilliantly lit from some point above the door, was covered by an oriental carpet of rare quality. Immediately opposite him was an open doorway, and to the side of it a single square window. A blind of some thin red material, through which a warm light glowed, was drawn down. It was clear that the fiddle-player was in the room behind the blind. In the open doorway, face to face with Plimsoll, stood a tall girl, "the most beautiful I ever set eyes on." Her long hair was let down and she was stark-naked. Plimsoll's enjoyment of this rather surprising view, and of the heavenly music that went with it, was exceedingly brief, for as he pushed the door open with his right hand, a stiletto flashed at him from the left, ripping away a strip of cloth from the front of his waistcoat. Plimsoll stepped back, pulling the door after him, and retreated into the busy market-street.

In 1914, to miss assassination in Soho by a hair's breadth was quite a thing, and I was not surprised to learn that Plimsoll went off to look for a policeman. He found one in Piccadilly Circus and told the man his story. But the policeman was not sympathetic. He told Plimsoll that by opening closed doors and poking his nose into other people's business he was "asking for it," and let it be a lesson to him. Besides, he could not leave his beat. Eyetalians, Plimsoll might be sure.

I think it was the quality of the violin-playing and the rarity of the carpet in that squalid little courtyard which most puzzled Plimsoll. That so exquisite a creature as the girl should have had a jealous protector of her nudity, quick with a dagger, did not strike him as so peculiar. And I had not the heart to hint that had the assassin with the stiletto held his hand for a split second, until something more than the intruder's waistcoat came into view, he might not have lunged at all. Within his frail coxswain's body Plimsoll was very much a man, fit target for a jealous Neapolitan lover, and it would have been unkind to suggest that he might, if more fully exposed to view, have been spared.

## CHAPTER XII

# BOBBY WHITE'S BOX

MOST men could manage to look soldierly after the First World War, but there was still something, a touch of innocence perhaps, that distinguished a member of the old regular Army from the rest of us. Certainly Brigadier-General the Hon. Robert White, when he became a stockbroker in the nineteen-twenties, still looked like a regular soldier, with all the candour, the trustfulness, the aptitude for being ambushed by the facts of life, that clung to army men who had fought the Boers. He could even put on that knowing look, head slightly inclined to one side, that simple souls are apt to assume, as if to protect their own simplicity. There was an engaging slyness about Bobby at times, a little shake of the head, to indicate, even though subconsciously, that he was after all quite a downy old bird. Of course the Stock Exchange took him to its heart, and I have been told that he was shadowed there by a confidential clerk, who would approach a jobber after Bobby had made a verbal bargain. "You understand, of course, that when our General White said 'an eighth' he meant 'five-eighths'?" And the jobber understood, and altered the figure in his book. It is pleasant to know that, with Bobby, manifest goodness had its reward. In a decade or so Bobby made a modest fortune on which to retire, with leisure to ride his favourite hobby-horse, which was to walk alone the Highland glens, with map and book, and to fight again, in his mind's eye, the miniature but miraculous battles of Montrose.

Nobody would have guessed, in those later years, that this eager, friendly man had once worn the broad arrow in one of His Majesty's Prisons, and had been dismissed from the Army. Yet so it was, for young Captain White had been with Jameson in "the Raid," had been captured at Doornkop on that fatal New Year's Day; had been sent home, with his leader, to be tried and imprisoned for making war on a State with whom Queen Victoria was at peace.

Bobby, who was reinstated in the Army and commanded a brigade in the First World War, did not often care to talk about the days of his public disgrace, and of one episode he never spoke at all. This affair became known as that of "Bobby White's box," and Bobby's permanent silence about it was an act of generosity of which few men but he would have been capable. The story is this. After the surrender at Doornkop there fell into the hands of the Boers a despatch-box containing the codes in use between the Raiders and the Reform Committee in Johannesburg, as well as lists of the conspirators and other incriminating papers. On the box was painted, in large letters, "Capt. R. White." Now, from the time when the white flag was raised by Jameson's little band, to the time when the Boers took over their baggage, there had been ample space for all these papers to be destroyed. To have allowed them to fall into Boer hands was an act of gross and culpable stupidity. And this folly, when the facts about the box and the papers came out, was naturally imputed to the

owner of the box. The Boers made full use of their
windfall, and *De trommel van Bobby White* became
legendary among them. And not only among them:
Bobby White had the chagrin, on a chance encounter
with Sir Douglas Haig in France in 1916, of being
greeted with: "Hello Bobby! Any more trommels?"

To clear himself completely Bobby White needed
only to tell the simple truth: that his box had been
borrowed, when Bobby himself was away on a mission,
by his commanding officer. But for thirty-five years he
held his tongue. So did the real culprit. While one man
preferred to be unjustly written down an ass rather than
exonerate himself at the expense of another, that other
was content to let it be so. Not until after the death of
this too reticent soldier did the truth come out, through
a letter to *The Times* from a brother-officer, who had
watched the packing of the secret papers by his own, and
Bobby's, C.O. This brother-officer, Colonel J. B.
Stracey-Clitheroe, had protested, in vain, against the
carrying of such dangerous matter into action: "If we
don't get through," said the C.O., "we shall all be shot,
so what does it matter?"

Thirty-five years of silence under a false imputation
would have been signally magnanimous in anybody;
in Bobby I think it shines with a particular lustre. For it
is harder to be accused of a fault of which you might
conceivably be capable than of one of which you are
incapable. And I have a suspicion that it could not have
been said of Bobby, with absolute assurance, that in no
circumstances could he have lost his head. He was, for
instance, a keen deer-stalker, but not a very successful
one. For Bobby suffered from what is known as "stag-
fever"; at the crucial moment, when his target was

within range and standing broadside on, Bobby's tremulous excitement would be such that he lost control of his muscles, and could not steady himself for the shot. Now we know something of what happened at Doornkop after the white flag had been raised. And to a gallant, emotional, idealistic young officer such as Bobby, it must have been a bitter and moving experience. Might not a temperament which could betray him over the slight matter of taking aim at a stag have also played him false in so momentous and desperate affair as a surrender? Is not some cool strain of calculation required in a man who is to remember a bundle of papers at a moment of failure and humiliation? Bobby was the most emotional of men. To watch his face at a play was to see reflected in it everything that was taking place on the stage. His expressive and mobile features frowned or smiled, threatened or pleaded, with each actor or actress in turn. He was a man of feeling, of enthusiasm, of sympathies, of excitements. I believe that although Bobby did not forget, yet he could have forgotten, those precious papers.

I am sure that he knew himself. His straightforward mind was not the sort to nourish illusions. If I am right, if Bobby could have said of the negligent officer, "There but for the grace of God goes Robert White," then, it seems to me, his conduct was so much the more admirable. There is a pride, a private self-regard, which can sustain of its own strength the assaults of undeserved censure. I doubt if it was a pride of this sort that prompted Bobby's unpublished generosity. Rather do I think it came from something rarer and finer still, the golden gift of fellow-feeling.

## CHAPTER XIII

# FOX-STALKING

I SHOULD say at once that fox-stalking, unlike deer-stalking in Scotland, is not one of these so-called "blood sports" to which so many birds and animals are indebted for their easy, happy, sheltered lives. The object of fox-stalking, as once practised by myself, was to get near enough to a wild fox to touch him with the hand. I did not succeed, but I did get within three feet of him, and had I been carrying a cane, could have surprised him with a gentle poke.

The idea no doubt came to me because I had been deprived, by an operation on an old wound, from my usual Scottish holiday. Instead, I was spending most of August and September at Westonbirt, that immense sham-Jacobean pile in Gloucestershire which atoned, by its rare or stately trees, its wide lawns, its great pictures, its nectarines and peaches, for the embarrassing ostentation of Vulliamy's designs. It was one of those too few late-summers when day follows day with unbroken sunshine; the gardens where I spent my days had those broad expanses of smooth-shaven lawn which, English above all else, give a feeling of civilised security; white flannels flickered in the distant nets whence came the click of bat on ball; and, morning and evening, peace was proclaimed by the ceaseless, but infinitely caressing, voices of the wood-pigeons. As a Norfolk child I had been taught to interpret their reiterated recitative as, "My toe bleeds, Betty," and it is possible, no doubt, to hear complaint in that short, heavily accented, phrase; but personally I have long since left off thinking of bleeding toes, or of any kind of grievance, when I hear a wood-pigeon coo. To my ear nothing can be more soothing and encouraging, from that first sudden vehemence in courting-time, to the calm, meditative utterances of late summer evenings, when the shadows of the shocks are long upon the stubbles, the rabbits sit humped in the yellow sunshine, and the rooks begin to come home.

As I still had an open wound that needed professional dressing, I was shadowed by my slim and gentle nurse, Sister Iris Partridge, and for a week or two listened to the wood-pigeons only from the Italian garden, where I attempted to paint in oils, for I had been given a couple of lessons by Mrs Graham-Smith at Easton Grey, nearby. Lucy Graham-Smith was a cripple, and a sister of Margot Asquith, of whom she was an expurgated edition. For she had all Margot's warm heart, and much of her lively mind, without the impetuosity and occasional childishness of her famous sister. She showed me how to prepare my paints, how to hold a brush, and watched me, stroke by stroke, paint a green and brown jug with a blob of white pigment for the highlight. I was then turned loose in the garden. I belonged to the strictly representative school of landscape painting. I not only tried to imitate what I saw, but used my knowledge of what I could not see: that the surfaces, for instance, reflecting colour to my eyes, were not all on the same plane, but arranged in depth. The result was exceedingly dull and uninteresting. Had not Sister Partridge gallantly volunteered to wash my brushes after each session in soap and water, an intolerably wearisome chore, but one insisted on by my teacher, I should not have long persevered in art. As it was, I painted two pictures in all, a garden landscape and a full-length portrait of my kind nurse.

But my heart was in the Highlands, and by the time the portrait was finished I was feeling stronger, and anxious to be trying out my muscles. So we began to wander further afield, and on one of these strolls I first saw the foxes. There were three of them, a vixen and two cubs, almost as large as herself, playing together at the edge of a wood. The vixen lay at length in the grass and the cubs rolled about her; there was some shadow-boxing, and snarling; then all three shammed dead for a bit and came to life again as one fox. It was a charming sight, and the play went on for so long, at about a hundred yards' range from where we stood at a gate, and the foxes seemed so confident and unalert, that I began to examine the terrain with a view to making a nearer approach. By a wide detour we could have got into the wood, out of which the foxes had broken into the sunny meadow, but the wood was thick with under-growth, and to approach from inside it without snapping a stick or making a warning rustle would have been out of the question. So then I remembered South Uist, and the early-morning crawls after Grey Lag geese. Compared to those, deer-stalking on the high hills is child's play, for the geese feed on dead flat ground, post a sentinel to keep watch, and must be approached to within gun-shot, not rifle-shot. There may be a stone wall, or a ditch, to give cover, but more often there are only the slightest depressions and irregularities in the

ground, or clumps of herbage, rush, or heather on its
surface. Wriggling, face down, with a sense of grievance
that a being made in God's image should have so jutting
a posterior, is the usual method of approach for a goose-
stalker.

So when something had disturbed the foxes and they
had retreated into cover, I walked over the rough
meadow between our gate and the wood, surveying it
with a goose-stalker's eye. There were thistles; there
were clumps of rushes and of higher herbage where, no
doubt, manure had been deposited; there were minor
undulations in the soil itself, shallow runnels and corru-
gations. I lay down here and there and decided that it
would "go." But would the vixen and her cubs come
back another day?

They did come back, and almost to the same spot, so
that my survey became serviceable. But first I had to
overcome the scruples of my nurse, who took the view
that a hundred and twenty yards' wriggle would not
only exhaust her convalescent, but be certain to dis-
arrange the dressings that covered an unhealed wound.
However, by arguing that there is no position so restful
as the recumbent one; that I would work by short shifts
interrupted by long spells of immobility, and, finally,
that the chances against my getting more than thirty
yards were exceedingly slender, I won my point. If the
bandages shifted, I promised to abandon the stalk.

The foxes were playing unconcernedly when I lay
down at the far edge of the field to begin my wriggle.
A tree behind them in the wood gave me my direction.
Obedient to my nurse, I took my time; indeed, I was
compelled to do so, by sheer lack of training and short-
ness of breath. But in thinking that the stalk would be

called off before I had crawled the whole distance, I had been mistaken. I had overlooked the fact that, once down to the wriggle, I should not dare raise my head to take a peep at the quarry. For more than half of my slow and worm-like progress I was under the impression that Sister Partridge was watching the foxes from behind a stone wall, and that her silence proved that they were still undisturbed. So far I had not even ventured to look behind me, lest raising my face from the turf should expose some part of my head. But having reached a clump of nettles about forty yards from my objective, I was able to look back. Sister Partridge had not stayed behind a stone wall; she lay, face down, like a dead nurse, not twenty yards behind me. She had had no faith, either in her bandages, or in my promise to desert if they went wrong. Determined to be on hand in case of mishap, yet unwilling to spoil my fun, she had gallantly wormed and squirmed, regardless of clothes and silk stockings, in my tracks. I should have been touched and grateful. I was neither; I was furious. Not only had the risk of failure been doubled, but the chances were that for half an hour or more we had both been stalking nothing. That so cunning an animal as a vixen, with two grown cubs as adjutants, should allow a man to trek up to her was improbable, but that she should permit a man and a hospital nurse, who had never stalked a Grogarry goose in her life, to do so, seemed impossible. When the apparently dead nurse raised a cautious eye from the grass, I made minute but angry gestures to convey to her both my displeasures and an order to stay put. Ever docile, she flattened herself like a plaice on the sea-bottom. I went on with my slow, tedious crawl, but as a man without hope. When I reached the spot, a few yards from the edge of the wood, where I judged the foxes to have been playing, I warily raised my head. About a yard away lay a fox, whether the vixen or one of the cubs I cannot be sure. With a stick I could have touched her; I attempted to do so with an outstretched arm. She leapt to her feet and bounded to the edge of the wood. There she turned to face me. Everything in her attitude expressed astonishment, except her eyes, which were soulless, cold and empty. In a second she was gone.

I must admit that I was as surprised to see only one fox as that fox was to see me. Had I found all three, relaxed at their games, I should have been less astonished. But that two should have cleared off, leaving one unsuspicious, is, I think, remarkable. On the whole I am inclined to think that the animal I so nearly touched must have been a cub, too innocent, too green, to guess why the others had decamped.

I am not prepared, on the strength of this one experience, to recommend fox-stalking as a sport. But if anyone should feel moved to emulation, and should succeed, as I did not, in touching a fox, fairly stalked for a hundred and twenty yards across a flat field, with their hand, I would like to say now that I shall not consider myself bested unless my rival can produce a certificate that he was accompanied, at twenty paces to the rear for three-quarters of the distance, by a fully qualified hospital nurse wearing her best silk stockings.

## CHAPTER XIV

# FOR BIRD-LOVERS ONLY

THERE are, nowadays, columns in many of the daily papers which follow, at a great distance, in the footsteps of the mighty Beachcomber. When the harassed author of one of these runs out of ideas, he can always safely fall back upon a paragraph that guys bird-lovers. There ought not to be anything comic about a liking for birds, but, to the public at large, there demonstrably is. It can hardly be that birds themselves are felt to be funny. The joke is partly that supposedly serious and adult people should waste so much time watching, thinking and talking about creatures which have so little use, and partly the names given to birds. To write of a Lesser Mottled Grass-chat is, for some reason, to make a sure hit. For the name-joke ornithologists themselves may be partly to blame. People who call the Manx Shearwater *Puffinus puffinus*, while the Puffin himself is fobbed off with *Fratercula Arctica* can hardly expect to escape a few gibes.

But bird-lovers, of whom I count myself one, are not to be put off by the crackling of thorns under a pot. The sum of pleasurable moments (some fleeting as the flash of a kingfisher) which the sight and sound of birds add to the enjoyments of a lifetime is not to be despised. They can be the accompaniment of many other out-of-door pursuits. The long waits by covert or hedgerow

call for no patience when enlivened by glimpses of the
unique family-feeling of long-tailed tits, the mouselike
spirallings of a tree-creeper, or the noiseless flitting of a
brown owl. The frustrations of the mediocre golfer can
often be soothed by the cry of the green plover, or the
bubbling of curlew when spring is on the way. And the
man in the corner of the third-class railway carriage who
nudged his *vis-à-vis* with his knee and said: "Look at
them bloody rooks," was, lover or not, at least temper-
ing his boredom with a glance at the birds.

And once in a while the birds can present the watcher
with a spectacle so improbable, so unexpected and so
lordly, that not even the most hardened scoffer could
forbear, if not to cheer, at any rate to stand silent and
admire. Such a spectacle came my way once, in the
foothills of the Pyrenees, and because it was so rare, as
well as beautiful, I think it worth recording. For its
rarity I have the word, not only of the books, but of
little bearded Dr Blazy, of St Jean-de-Luz, who had
been in his time a great vulture-hunter, seeking out these
majestic but rather scruffy and sinister creatures in the
high places of the Pyrenees.

I found myself in that romantic countryside, and
acquainted with little Dr Blazy, for the same reason;
that I had been ordered abroad to convalesce, after a
serious illness. St Jean-de-Luz, said the doctors, because
of the mildness of the climate; but I do not think they
can have been there themselves to see the ominous
growth of ferns on the limbs of all the trees. As the
Norfolk widow remarked after her husband, dead these
twenty yenrs, had appeared to her, sitting in his own
armchair and solid as life: "They du say that means
rain"; and rain, five days out of seven, was what these

ferns did in fact presage. In a way it was just as well, for having with me my whole family, my nurse, dear Sister Margaret Conley, and "Batey," an Oxford hockey-blue, as man-governess for my elder daughters, I had taken a large villa on the hills behind Ciboure for the sake of the view, forgetting to enquire about the water-supply. Only after the contract was signed did we discover that there was none, except rain-tanks. For drinking-water we had to depend on a spring in a near-by ravine; but the rain, warm and persistent, kept us in baths.

But on the two days a week when the sun shone, and especially after the southern spring had begun its work of embellishment, we used to be driven, with a picnic lunch, up to a certain high *col* where a minor road crossed the frontier into Spain. A pair of French, and a pair of Spanish, frontier-guards lounged by their small guardhouses, but took little notice of us, and whether we spread the old plaid rug on the Spanish or the French side of the watershed was a matter decided by the wind, not by passports. It was a little way downhill on the Spanish slopes, where the hillside was a patchwork of *maquis*, clearings of rough grass, and sudden outcrops of rock, that we first saw the rare birds. They were circling, a pair of them, with no visible motion of their great rigid wings, on a level with ourselves. They were enormous, and, at a first glance, white as snow. They appeared to be quartering the broken ground beneath them with patient intensity. They must have seen, but did not condescend to notice, ourselves, our rugs or our baskets. On their nearer approach, we could discern, without binoculars, the mourning-bands that tipped and edged their snowy pinions, and the pale yellow of their heads. They were Egyptian Vultures.

We had already seen, more than once, although at a far greater distance, the rusty black Griffon Vultures, and knew, from their size, that these shining white birds must be vultures too. But I had never, in those days, heard of a white vulture, and it seemed strange that Dr Blazy, in our many conversations while he was preparing his syringe, had never mentioned them. It turned out later that in all his mountain expeditions, over many years, he had never once had a glimpse of these rarities, and that, though he knew of their existence in the high Pyrenees, they were so much in the back recesses of his mind that he had not thought to speak of them. When he did hear, not only that we had seen them, but watched them at close quarters for a couple of hours or more, and not merely circling and soaring as great white lords of the air, but coming down to earth, there to suffer moments of almost comic humiliation, his envy and jealousy were a pleasure to watch. For these Egyptians must have been after something that afternoon, low down as they were in the foothills, since they circled persistently over the selfsame area, alighting at intervals to rest on an outcrop within a couple of hundred yards of our picnic. But rest was denied to them; for no sooner had they perched than a pair of ravens, not half their size, began to mock them. These two black tormentors hopped and flapped about the great birds, making darts at them, like Shallow's "little quiver fellow," who "would about, and about, and come you in, and come you in: 'rah, tah, tah,' would he say; 'bounce' would he say, and away again would he go, and again would he come." There could be no better description than Shallow's of the way these two ravens plagued the majestic pair, who, as a result, lost a good deal of face in our eyes. For when sitting on a rock they did assume that hunched, vulturine look which has more of patience than pride in it; also they were clumsier on their feet than the ravens, and shuffled and shifted rather inelegantly when attacked. Not that they showed any real fear; there was no question of their being driven away or put off the business in hand; nor did they bother to counter-attack. But they did allow themselves to be worried and teased, and considering their size and weight, and the splendour of their looks on the wing, we were disappointed in them. It was a relief to us as well as to them when the ravens, tired of the game, departed, and the vultures, once again airborne, resumed their sedulous and unhurried sweeping. But at length it must have become clear to them that they were on a wild-vulture chase, for they began to soar, and making height with no perceptible wing-beats, the bright birds rose, in diminishing spirals, to be lost to sight in the eastern sky.

I went down the hill in the hope of finding some reason for what was, as Dr Blazy later assured me, a most unusual visitation. And perhaps I did find it; for in one of the grassy clearings I came upon a mare grazing close to a newly-dropped foal. From all appearances the damp little creature, looking all legs and still unable to stand, must have been born during the afternoon. Had the vultures spotted the mare in labour and hoped, vulture-like, for a stillbirth? It seems possible.

The surprise and pleasure of that afternoon have stayed with me, as has the visit to our villa garden of a flock of siskins, filling the treetops with a noise like the ringing of fairy bicycle-bells, and my first view, also in that garden, of a woodchat and an Icterine warbler.

But on another occasion the sight of an exciting stranger led to exasperation as well as delight. It was a few years later, at Château d'Oeux, above the Lake of Geneva. I was again hunting for a cure—and this time successfully—at Lausanne, and had taken a day off to visit a friend in that higher hinterland. In a hayfield, close to the hotel, my eye was caught by a flash of orange, black and white. The small, short-tailed bird who flaunted these gaudy colours obligingly perched on a telegraph-wire, and there broke into a song, as brilliant as, but more continuous than, a blackcap's. I had my binoculars; the bird was tame: and I was able to go back to the hotel and make a coloured sketch of this attractive little singer, with his bright contrasting colours all correctly delineated. I then sent the drawing to one of our best-known field-naturalists who was, I think, serving with the League of Nations at Geneva and had lately published some account of the birds of Switzerland.

In due course I received his reply. It was written with the patient kindness of an aunt whose small nephew has described a fairy seen on the roof of the potting-shed. There was no such bird in Switzerland; my observation must have been at fault; perhaps what I had seen was a this, conceivably a that (naming two inconspicuous species known to me). It was infuriating. On my return to London, I took my sketch to the Natural History Museum. A courteous young man in spectacles glanced at my sketch, said he could not name the bird offhand, but had no doubt he would be able to identify it from so competent a drawing. He dropped no hint about fairies. The following day he wrote to me that the bird was a well-known Brazilian songbird, regularly exported to Europe in cages, being valued for its bright colours and attractive singing. My bird at Château d'Oeux must have been an "escape"; a possibility that had escaped, as the bird its cage, the mind of the naturalist whom I had first consulted.

But since my powers of observation had been vindicated, and because his letter had been kind as well as crushing, I did not bother to point this out to Mr Anthony Buxton.

So much for my own encounters with rare birds. But before leaving a subject so distasteful to many, so captivating to a few, I cannot refrain from re-telling a tale told me long ago by my father. His story was that in a year which, after consulting Howard Saunders's *Manual of British Birds*, I think must have been 1870 or 1871, the Ambassador of a European power was staying at Wilton House for a pheasant-shoot. At the end of the first day's shoot, his host, Lord Pembroke, found himself in a quandary. For the Ambassador, during a day which he had greatly enjoyed, had managed to hit, as makeweight for all too few pheasants, a number of beaters, keepers and guests, not to speak of badly frightening those whom he had missed or spared. There had been, fortunately, no serious wounding; but all concerned, including the host, were inwardly resolved not to risk another day of such peppering. But how to eliminate from among the guns one who, as well as being the most dangerous, the most important and the keenest, must on no account be offended? International, as well as personal, repercussions had to be considered.

This problem, it must be supposed was preoccupying Lord Pembroke as he sipped his port-wine and listened to the great man's eulogies of the past, and hopes for the next, day's sport. But after dinner he had what is called a lucky break. In one of the stately corridors that led from dining-room to drawing-room stood a row of immense glass cases containing some immense stuffed birds. The Ambassador was greatly struck by their size, their lordly stance, their unusual moustaches. "And what," he asked, "are these splendid creatures?"

"Great Bustards."

"Great, indeed. And where were they shot?"

"Out there, on the Plain."

"One killed those monsters here, at Wilton?"

"Certainly."

"Ah!—if I could but shoot one of these, how happy I should be!"

Lord Pembroke's mind, sharpened by his predicament, worked quickly. Did he put his finger to his lips, or merely wink, behind His Excellency's back, at his other guests? However that may be, he did not hesitate. Nor did he tell the eager foreigner that the last Great Bustard had been killed on Salisbury Plain at least sixty years ago.

"Would you care to try for one tomorrow?"

"It would be my greatest happiness."

"Then it shall be arranged."

And it was. Next morning the shooting party, with relief, tinged, one hopes, with remorse, watched His Excellency, followed by pack-ponies slung with panniers, ride gaily out to scour the Plain for Bustard. They shot their pheasants in peace and safety. And when dusk fell, as they were returning to the house, they saw the little cavalcade come back. But there was no gaiety now. The Ambassador, so jaunty after breakfast, was humped wearily on his tired mount. He looked exhausted and depressed. His host, smothering self-reproach, hailed him cheerfully.

"Well, Ambassador, had a good day?"

"Alas, no. Miles and miles have we ridden on your Plain; and only shot three birds."

Only three Great Bustards: the first to be seen in Wiltshire since 1810. Lord Pembroke and his guests must have had some difficulty in assuming the appropriate expressions of concern.

Such was the story as I had it from my father. And now, for truth's sake, I must reluctantly add that when, not long since, I was taken to see Wilton House and had an opportunity of asking Lord Pembroke if family tradition preserved the tale, he said No. The story was new to him. But who could have invented so circumstantial an account of so unlikely an incident? That the Great Bustard became extinct on Salisbury Plain in "the first decade of the Nineteenth Century," but that "a considerable number" visited this country in the winter of 1870–71 (and "a smaller migration" in 1889–90) is confirmed by Howard Saunders. May not a true adventure, as so often happens, have become attached to the wrong background? Any tale of distinguished Ambassadors and Salisbury Plain is likely, in the end, to be fathered upon Wilton House. But may there not be other houses within reach of the Plain, capable of sheltering at once a stuffed Bustard and a diplomat? I cling to the hope that, if only by this re-telling, so well-found a tale may be helped to recover its wavering authenticity.

## CHAPTER XV

# IN THE SOUND OF SLEAT

"THIS place is so beautiful that it makes you ache," wrote Sidney Peel from Armadale Castle in the Isle of Skye, and those who know the west coast of Scotland can well understand what he meant. I knew it already, for I had stayed at Arisaig with Sir Arthur Nicholson and his family, who are my cousins, and had seen that tawny riband of seaweed which frames the fretted coastline like a passe-partout of old gold. And from a rocky promontory I had heard for the first time that mysterious half-human cooing, suggesting the conversation of a bevy of Lady Violet Bonham-Carters, which I suspected to be the voices of mermaids but discovered to be those of the eider-duck. At Arisaig I had shot woodcock and heard my host recall how he had seen a famous cricketer lay down his gun and field a low-flying woodcock with his hands. He also liked to tell of his notable right-and-left, a snipe and a camel, for which he had to pay heavily, barely escaping with his life from the indignant fellaheen, whose camel it was that lurked so expensively among the tall bulrushes. I could not then cap his feat with that of my instructor at a shooting-school at Wembley who, wandering with his shotgun on a wide no-man's-land near Salonika, had flushed simultaneously a woodcock and a Turk. He bagged the Turk, whose own aim with a heavier rifle

was a fraction too leisurely, with his first barrel, and the
woodcock with his second. But this is shameless
digression.

A visit to Sidney and Delia Peel, the wise and the gay,
would have been memorable in Bermondsey: at
Armadale Castle, facing across the Sound of Sleat those
incomparable contours of the forest of Knoidart, it was
unforgettable. It is true that I nearly embroiled my host
with his landlord by referring at the tea-table, through a
slip of the tongue, to one of the fishing gillies as
"Macleod," for the youthful heir of the Macdonalds,
a freckled twelve-year-old, was a guest at the tea-table,
and at the sound of that detested name he leant forward
over his plate, red in the face and all but shouting: "We
have no Macleods here!" Sidney hastened to assure the
young gamecock that the gillie was a Mac-something
neutral and harmless, and I, who had been a frequent
guest, although not at Dunvegan Castle, of the Macleod
of Macleod himself, was under the necessity, for my
host's sake, of holding my tongue, much as I should have
liked to scourge the small barbarian for his insupportable
and artificial ferocity.

But what I set out to tell was the incident of the
mackerel. A few of us had embarked in a light boat for
an evening row in the Sound, without fishing-tackle
and with no particular purpose beyond that of enjoying
the colour and mystery of the mountains on the main-
land. The sea was calm, the air windless, and the
appearance, on more than one bearing at once, of
travelling catspaws suddenly darkening and ruffling the
surface of the sea, caught our attention. But there was
something unusual about these disturbances; for one
thing they were moving, although by no means far

apart, in different directions; for another their texture was quite unlike that of a water-ruffle made by wind: the sea was not corrugated, but pitted like the damp sand of a bunker in which sheep have been sheltering; the surface appeared to be stabbed from below, and, strangest of all, a myriad silvery drops were rising and falling over the whole of each separate area of turbulence. Even the gillie who was with us betrayed surprise, then made up his mind: "Yon are mackerel."

We had no rod with us, but I had an ash walking-stick; someone produced string, and the gillie bent a piece of wire into a hook. But what to do for bait? "Anything that's white" said the gillie, and I was about to tear a pocket-handkerchief when the gillie cut a curl from the coat of a white-and-yellow dog, a shaggy spaniel, who was of the party. By this time the course of one of those moving patches, like some gigantic Pool of Siloam in which the Angel was busy, lay across our bows, and we rowed hard to intercept it. It had a front of about fifty yards, and a length of a hundred at least, and as we drew near, we saw that what had appeared from afar as silver drops, were in fact shoals of tiny fishes, leaping to escape the mackerel. They rose and fell like the spray of a wind-blown fountain, while their devourers stabbed and churned the surface below them. We rowed our boat into the middle of the threshing shoal, dropped the small white bunch of dog's hair, tightly bound to the wire hook, over the gunwale, and immediately hooked a fish. A lift of the walking-stick jerked the catch into the boat, to be deftly disengaged by the gillie; a second drop of the hook, and the unappetising lure was again taken instantaneously. So excited and voracious were the mackerel that not once was there hesitation or rejection; we had but to drop the hook overboard to catch a fish there and then. It was in no sense sport, but what with the swirl and hiss of the sea around us, the frenzied leaping of the small fry, the sensuous thrill of feeling the tug and waggle of a fish at the end of a line, be it only a string on a stick, there was no lack of excitement. Moreover, taking sides—as who would not?—with the pursued against the pursuers, we had the sense of being in some sort, if not rescuers, at any rate avenging angels. So when one shoal had passed by, we rowed hard for another; when the first curl was worn out, the dog cheerfully obliged with a second; and not until the hunters, swifter in their mad pursuit than our clumsy boat, had boiled away beyond our reach did we row for the shore. And here we saw the most surprising thing of all, a sight which the gillie declared he had never before seen or even heard spoken of. The rocks lapped by the sea were brindled, as if by a light sprinkling of snow, by the bodies of the tiny fish who, driven landwards by their implacable hunters, had leapt ashore to flop and perish and whiten the shore-line. In their frantic terror, hundreds of these little creatures had hurled themselves several yards upwards and forwards. It was Skye, not a cloud, that had a silver lining that day. If St Francis ever preached to the mackerel, which are found in the Mediterranean, he must have wasted his breath: if to their victims, he is likely to have had a sullen and sceptical congregation.

On arrival at the landing-place, the catch filled several buckets, and, good as a mackerel can be with fennel sauce, we decided that one bucketful would satisfy the inhabitants of Armadale Castle. We proposed, accordingly, to distribute the rest throughout the village, but the gillie explained that mackerel are held by the people of Skye to be unfit for human consumption. It was not that they dislike the taste, for they have never tasted them: their antipathy is due to an ancient superstition that mackerel feed on the bodies of drowned sailors. So there we were, guilty of having killed for killing's sake; while the crofters, scratching a bare living from a shallow and grudging soil, turned up their noses at a sea-harvest, at once wholesome, plentiful, and to be reaped with an inch of bent wire and the hairs of a dog.

## CHAPTER XVI

# PITFALLS

HAT actions can be highly misleading, unless the
motive that prompted them is known, we all
know. A celebrated case is that of Mr Gladstone
who was on occasions seen to be conversing with
prostitutes; since the viewers were out of earshot, they
could not hear that earnest moralist's impassioned plea
for repentance and amendment, and so drew the wrong
conclusion. A minor example of the same sort, also
affecting a great Liberal statesman, illustrates how hard
it must be for public men never to put a foot wrong,
even in private.

I have an old friend, a General, a salty and original
character. In one of those conversations over the port
in which Generals are at their best and mellowest, the
soldier in him got the better of the Tory, and he
declared that this country never had a better Minister
at the War Office than Lord Haldane. When enlarging,
with the authority of one who has always made his
profession his first care, upon the foresight shown by
Haldane before 1914, both in the plan for a Territorial
Army and in his insistence on having two divisions
trained and equipped to take the field on the day of
mobilisation, he spoke of the War Minister in terms of
the greatest admiration and respect. So it was a surprise
to me when, having finished his eulogy, he leant back,

re-filled his glass, and said: "Pity the man was such a cad."

Now if the General had said: "Pity the man was a Liberal," or "Pity he joined the Labour Party," I could have understood it, but "cad" applied to Lord Haldane, and uttered by one who accuses nobody loosely, fell strangely upon the ear. I had never met Lord Haldane personally, but I had heard his character discussed by his intimates, such as Sir Edward Grey and Miss Violet Markham, and a less "caddish" person than this bulky and brooding philosopher, magnanimous and humane, it would be hard to imagine. I reacted sharply. "Haldane a cad? What do you mean?"

"I'll tell you. I wouldn't have believed it myself if I hadn't seen it. I was dining one night with dear old Robin Benson. Haldane was the chief guest. After the ladies had gone, Haldane moved up and sat on Robin's right. The butler brought round some cigars, several boxes of them, and Haldane, after a good deal of picking and feeling, selected one and lit it. Would you believe it, after three or four puffs, and without a word to his host, he stuck it in a tumbler and beckoned to the butler. Not good enough for him!—and, by George, you know the kind of cigars Robin used to keep. Tip-top. The butler brought another box, Haldane picked a second cigar, lit it, and, believe it or not, after a couple of puffs or so, stuck that one in the tumbler with the first! You never saw such a thing. Back comes the butler and this time dumps three or four boxes all round Haldane: well, you'll hardly credit it, but I tell you the fellow tried at least five, if not six, cigars, and stuck 'em in the tumbler before he found one to his taste. And all as cool as be damned. It made my blood boil—dear old Robin sitting there at his own table and never batting an eyelid, whilst a guest waves his butler about and chucks away his priceless cigars like so many twopenny cheroots! It was the damnedest behaviour I ever saw. If a man who can do that isn't a cad, what is he I should like to know?"

By sheer good luck I was able to tell him. Years before, Robin Benson had once said to me: "Do you know who is the best judge of a cigar in London? Haldane. I would never dream of stocking up my cabinet until I had got Haldane to come and tell me which to buy. He's infallible. Just a puff or two at each, and he makes his choice. I suppose it's a gift, like tea-tasting."

The General is anything but a gossip, and, because of his great admiration for Lord Haldane in other respects, I feel sure that his private view of the great man's character was never broadcast. But it could well have been otherwise, had the observer from the bottom of the table been less discreet, or readier to pick up sticks with which to beat a political opponent. A "cad" legend might well have been launched and never caught up with. It is a curious reflection that Cabinet Ministers and public men generally would be well advised to add to their list of forbidden activities that of choosing cigars for a friend.

A different sort of misunderstanding, which merely caused irritation and snapping among certain high Civil Servants, was told me by the late Lord Robson of Jesmond. He was at that time Attorney-General in Asquith's Government, and I came to know him through my friendship with his son, Harold. All the family were delightful; they lived in those days at

8

Rackheath near Norwich, whither, in my bachelor days, Lady Robson, piquante and gay in spite of serious deafness, used sometimes to invite me. It was there that the youngest daughter, Diana, aged twelve, won five shillings from me by climbing a monkey-puzzle tree, from which she descended streaming with blood, her stockings torn to shreds, and there that Sir William, over the port-wine, told me the following incident.

The Prince of Wales (later King George V) was to make a speech on some State occasion, and Sir William was mildly surprised one busy day in Chambers to find among the papers laid out for him by his clerk a draft of the Prince's speech. This, it appeared, had been sent to him by the Colonial Office, but since the speech, like other royal speeches, was platitudinous and innocuous, touching nowhere on the Law or the Constitution, the Attorney-General concluded that it had been sent to him in error, and consigned it to the waste-paper basket. A few weeks went by; then came a call from the Colonial Office to say that time was getting short, and would the Attorney-General please return the royal speech with his comments without further delay. Sir William felt somewhat annoyed, and himself rang up the Colonial Secretary to explain that the speech had nothing to do with him and should never have been sent to him. An office enquiry was started: who was responsible for the blunder? At length a draft was discovered containing a marginal note in red ink: "Should there not be a reference to A.G.?" The note was initialled. The owner of the initials, himself of no mean standing, was sent for by his chief. What, he was asked, was this nonsense about referring to the Attorney-

General? The official seemed genuinely puzzled. His own marginal minute was shown to him. "Oh, that," he said. "Well, I thought it might be as well, on so solemn an occasion, if the Prince of Wales were to make some reference to Almighty God."

## CHAPTER XVII

# GOLF

MABEL MULHOLLAND, the exquisite friend of my youth, married to a "whole-time" player of games, used sometimes to wonder aloud whether God had intended His creature, Man, to spend its conscious hours in knocking a small white ball into a hole. I could see her point. The broad lawns that spread about Worlingham Hall were dotted with golf-balls, that lay there, plentiful as mushrooms in a bumper year, to enable A.J.M. to practise his mashie-shots without the exertion of following up the ball. In his middle years he profoundly shocked me by enunciating the, to me, pernicious heresy that golf was a better sport than shooting.

"When I go shooting," he said, "I may or may not get enough birds over me to keep me amused; it's a question of luck, the season and the weather; but when I go golfing, I can have as many shots as I like and nothing is left to chance."

To me a day's shooting was a romantic experience, full of sensuous delights, of sights and sounds and smells, as well as of expectation, suspense and climax, and it had never occurred to me to regard it as an amusement that stood or fell by the number of cartridges fired. And that so good a shot as my host, with a rich man's unlimited opportunities, should, while missing so little, be missing so much, seemed to me a kind of betrayal, almost a *gran rifuto*. So far was I from being persuaded by him, that my heart was hardened against golf.

There had been nothing in my earlier years to incline me towards the game. As a very small boy indeed I had trudged round Hempton Common while my father and the bearded Mr Curtis, both wearing scarlet blazers to scare an imaginary public out of their way, knocked little white balls into gorse-bushes. And after the game they sat with two other men at a green-baize table in the wooden hut which served as club-house, and talked and talked, while I, insufferably bored, fidgetted in a corner. There was no tablecloth on the table, nor cups, nor plates; not a bun was in sight, only a bulging water-jug and two glasses. I felt as desolate as I had felt when, awaking prematurely from my morning rest and peeping into the day-nursery, I saw no sign of dinner, only the nurses by the red table-cloth, busy with their work-baskets. There is an aridity, a dreariness about an unlaid table which I never could bear; and I think my enforced presence at a committee meeting of the Hempton Golf Club, unrefreshed by so much as a finger-biscuit, gave me an early prejudice against golf itself.

My first attempts to play the game, on the brand-new course at Valescure, were not such as to kindle ambition in me. The fairways, cut through the *maquis*, were narrow and stony; a few ancient warped clubs of my father's seemed to me most unhandy things with which to hit a ball, and, in spite of a few lessons from an English professional, I rarely managed to get the ball into the air. Nor had I at that time seen a golfer. My father and his friends were all hopeless rabbits, and there was nothing in our raw nine holes, except the exquisite views of mountain and sea between the stone pines, to attract good players. And when a school-friend, Julian Martin-Smith, came over for the day from Cannes, and displayed to my astonished eyes the ease and grace of a born golfer, I felt discouragement, not emulation. For if that was how a golf-ball should and could be hit, the game was clearly beyond me. I had my rowing to think about, and I did not persevere.

At Oxford I took against golf for quite other reasons. Accepting with heart and soul the stern traditions of the boat club that the things for which one rowed were the honour and renown of the college, I could envy, but never approve of, the men who went off with their clubs to enjoy themselves. It was all right for Archie Gordon, valuable oarsman as he might well have been, because he played golf for the University against Cambridge; besides, he was a Scot, for whom golf was less a game than a natural function. But when Eric Romilly and Compton-Bracebridge and a bunch of my familiars spent their afternoons having fun, and returned to eat crumpets without a tremor of conscience, I, who had been tubbing freshmen, felt that for all their charm they were essentially wasters. What good were they to the college? Men who were never in training!

But after going down from Oxford I began to soften towards golf. May it partly be that about this very time a new golf correspondent was beginning to write in *The Times* and in *Country Life*? A writer whose English was so impeccable, whose style so fluent, whose quotations so apt, that even those who cared nothing about the game found themselves irresistibly drawn to read him? How was it possible to side any longer with the "hitting-a-little-white-ball-into-a-hole" school of thought when golf matches and tournaments were being reported in terms that Homer might have envied? When Tolley was always "majestic," when Miss Wethered was the "illustrious lady," when it could be written of a fine swinger of a golf-club that he must have had a beautiful tune running in his head, when even the tune could be identified as a hymn-tune:

> Happy birds that soar and fly,
> Round Thy altars, O Most High,

how could any reader continue to think of such a game, played by such lordly persons to the sound of such inward music, as anything but a noble one, made for heroes? I, for one, could not. Mr Bernard Darwin, making literature out of sport, did even more. He compelled us to believe that a golfer, fighting out the final of a championship in that most selfish of contests, a single at golf, was performing deeds that fell little short of heroic. I have no doubt whatever that, to be a great golfer, a man must have gifts of nerve, of temperament, of self-control, without which mere technical skill in hitting the little white ball would be of small avail. But it is not the high moral qualities of a Bobby Jones that Mr Darwin asks us to admire, nor his sheer skill either. In fact Mr Darwin asks us for nothing; rather he compels us to see Mr Bobby Jones as a paladin, a Roland, a gallant figure of romance, with his "brave" putts, his "daring" approaches, his "intrepid" recoveries. The word "glory" occurs as readily in Mr Darwin's reports of the contest for the President's Putter as in Napier's *History of the Peninsular War*. In short, Mr Darwin is a romantic, who has imagined a world of giants and splendour and, by the cunning of his pen, has made us believe in it too. His writing, call it what he may, is not reporting, it is creative. He has lifted a mere game to the level of chivalry, and made knightly tourneys out of stroke-competitions. And for his addicts there is no coming back to earth. His prose, readable to deceiving-point, sees to that. And how craftily he calls in aid the larks going up over Princes' at Sandwich, or the view of the Forth from Gullane Hill, to charm us into believing that the majestic Tolleys drew strength from their habitat! He weaves the landscape into the game, and all but credits a long, decisive putt to the sea-breezes of St Andrews. Or, like Milton, he intoxicates us with names, not of places or men but of holes and bunkers. Who, wherever English is spoken, has not heard of the Cardinal or the Principal's Nose? Who but Mr Darwin would venture to compare a solemn and silent contest between two courteous and self-controlled gentlemen to the snapping and worrying of curs? Yet "dog-fight" is one of his favourite words for describing just such a contest. And we accept it and believe in it.

Mr Darwin's accomplishment must surely be unique. He has not only devoted his life to playing a game and to writing about it; he has managed to convince us that his life has been well spent. For he has endowed that game with so much humanity, nature, bravery, even poetry, that it appears, when seen through his eyes, to satisfy most of the requirements of a civilised and manly life and the life, into the bargain, of an artist. It is a remarkable performance.

It would be too much to say that, but for Mr Darwin, I should never have taken up golf. There were concurrent social pressures. I began to feel out of things at a gay party, for instance, with the Asquith family at

Littlestone or Archerfield, when all the men and half
the girls went off to the links, and I alone was incom-
petent to join them. So I took lessons; I got the ball into
the air; I felt, now and then, the sensuous thrill of a well-
timed stroke; and although I have, through natural
ineptness, remained a rabbit for life, I count myself a
golfer. By a golfer I mean a man who can walk on to
the first tee of a strange course without feeling that he is
being watched from every window in the club-house.
(I do not include the first tee at Sandwich when White's
Club is holding its annual competition. With Lewis
Palmer I once found myself on that tee and on that
occasion; it was just after lunch; the members of
White's, in check tweeds, were drinking coffee on the
balconies; they looked like the well-fed tigers they
were; it was too much; I hit the ball with the toe of my
driver, and it cannoned off the sand-box into a clump of
marram-grass, and a roar of laughter went up behind
me of which the memory makes me wince to this
day.)

Once, and only once, have I played with a champion,
when I partnered the great Massy against the late Lord
Bicester on the little course at La Nivelle near St Jean
de Luz. Massy was an enormous, laughing man in a
blue beret, with gigantic hands. When I put him into a
thick bush of broom on the side of a bank he took a
niblick and uprooted the whole bush, which whirled
in the air, shedding pebbles and dirt, while the ball fell
plumb on the green a hundred yards away. But it was
on the greens that I first realised what it is to be a
champion. Massy holed out unfailingly from all over
the green; the sort of thing very small girls with an iron
twice as long as themselves can occasionally do, from

sheer ignorance of the difficulty of the feat, but otherwise none but champions.

Apart from Massy, and Mr Robert Gardiner, the American whom I watched in a semi-final of the Amateur Championship at Muirfield, I have seen few players of class. Nor am I a lucky spectator. When I went to Lord's to see Bradman he scratched about for a few balls and was bowled; and when once at Worplesdon my caddy nudged me: "Look! Miss Wethered," I turned to see a tall lady take an enormous divot instead of the ball. At a second attempt she topped it about fifty yards along the ground. I could hear her illustrious laughter across the intervening fairway, but she could not have caught my low groan, as I turned away in sorrow and dismay.

The late Lord Northcliffe was not at his best, either, when, at my sole encounter with that dictator, I played golf with him on his private course at Sutton Place. But when I say that, I am not thinking of his golf, for which he would have made no claims, but of his way of playing the host. For my wife and I had been invited by Lady Northcliffe, on a Sunday afternoon, to hear a famous singer. I wanted to hear the singing, and even more to explore that beautiful old house; but Lord Northcliffe intercepted us in the entrance-hall, and told me, a complete stranger, that since he had nobody with whom to play golf, I was to play a round with him. I pointed out that I had no clubs; that I was dressed in a tight blue suit and wore a starched collar and cuffs; that my shoes had smooth soles; in short that I was not dressed for golf, but for a concert. I even hinted politely that I should be very sorry to miss a rare musical occasion.

Lord Northcliffe overrode every objection. He would lend me some clubs; fresh air was worth all the music there was; golf could be played in any clothes (which, of the game as he played it, was true enough); and there was nobody else. I was by much his junior; I was his guest; I had to give in.

He produced a few clubs which, since there was no bag, I had to carry in a sheaf and glean after each stroke. On the way to the first tee we fell in with Arthur Steel-Maitland who, sharing his host's views about fresh air and music, had escaped from the drawing-room into the grounds. He was immediately conscripted to make up a threesome—less unwillingly, I think, than myself, for he was a rising Member of Parliament, and may well have felt, as he carried his own sheaf, that it embraced, like a lictor's rods, an invisible unground axe. Be that as it may, he and I remembered, as we reached the first tee, that although we had clubs of a sort, we had no golf-balls. We appealed to our host. Lord Northcliffe felt in his pockets and produced two new balls, wrapped up in tissue paper.

"I can sell you these," he said; "they are half a crown each."

"But I haven't got half a crown on me," said Steel-Maitland.

"You can borrow from Jones," said his Lordship.

Steel-Maitland, who had married money, did borrow from Jones (and forgot to repay); and I, who still counted my shillings, had to hand over five of them to that heavy, rich man on his own tee before a game into which I had been press-ganged could begin.

How the game ended I have forgotten. There was a small lake to be driven over, and Steel-Maitland drove into it and had to retire, for I had no more silver and our host carried no change. I rather think I won, in spite of my slippery shoes. Because of my tight clothes and the five bob, I felt rather peevish at the moment; but, looking backwards, I think the concert and the silver were well lost. After all, Lord Northcliffe was a great figure in his time and a remarkable man. And when I read about him, I see him before me: a massive head, carried low and pushed a little forward, with an overhanging lock of brown hair; a thick neck that weaved and shifted in a wide flannel collar; loose-hanging clothes of blue serge; a low, pleasant, gentle voice. I was nothing to him, but for all his insistence when "fagging" me, he was graciousness itself when selling me a Silver King.

When does a beginner become a golfer? Never, I think, until he has graduated from those delectable private park-courses, at Buckhurst, at Ford Manor, where the game got mixed up with flirtations (even, in my own case, with courtship) and trodden the firm, elastic turf of seaside links. I am not sure that I must not go further, and insist upon Scottish links, before true golferhood can be claimed. For when, as at Gullane Number One when I first knew it, the green-fee is one and sixpence a round, and your caddie costs you half a crown including the tip for cleaning your clubs, you know that you are in a land where golf is no longer a luxury or an amusement, but a necessity and a pursuit. You have only to watch the caddies swinging clubs as they wait for a customer, or to study their expressions of patient contempt when you pause at the top of Gullane Hill to exclaim at the breath-taking colours moving upon the hills of Fife, to become aware that you are no longer playing a rich man's game, but sharing in the serious pursuit of a serious people.

Not that, even in Scotland, the game is wholly democratic. If you looked eastward from Gullane Hill, during the breathers which even your caddie condoned if the couple in front were Princess Victoria and Lord Derby, you looked over Muirfield to Berwick Law. And Muirfield is not for everybody; the green-fee was ten shillings in those days, and you could only play there with an introduction from a Writer to the Signet or, as I did, as the guest of the great Sir John Fraser, the surgeon, who once saved my life. And by Berwick Law is the fashionable North Berwick, so crowded in those days that you must book a starting-time the day before you played a round. Yet even here there was egality: when the Grand Duke Michael of Russia went to book, and, giving his name, expressed a wish to start at ten o'clock, the starter did not so much as look up, but rapped out: "Ye'll starrt at eluvven-fufteen, and ye'll answer to the name of Macnab." So much for Grand Dukes.

But westward from Gullane Hill you could take your choice at one and sixpence; if the hill intimidated you, Gullane Number Two had gentler slopes; if you like to walk on the flatter, tamer ground, there was Luffness. And on the further horn of Aberlady Bay lies little Kilspindie, good for beginners, for it is short and unfrequented; but you must mark your ball well, even upon the fairways, for they are white with seagulls' feathers; why, I cannot tell. And you must have a care at the turn, not to break the windows of the grey, irregular stone house with the gables, for in it presided, in those far-away days, Mary, Lady Wemyss, that most valuable rarity, with whom you hoped to eat powdery three-cornered scones when the game was over. She never did, or could, disappoint you, unlike her guest, Sir James Barrie, who, on the only occasion I met him at her tea-table, uttered no single word from first to last. There were too many people present with whom he felt at home for me or any other stray visitor to take the blame: the little man with the great head was just not in the mood. So he munched away, looking sad and distinguished. There is good turf, for an inland course, at Gleneagles; and the Ochill Hills, that lie about it, are coated, like the South Downs, with pale grass, not heather, but their combes are steeper and their shadows more emphatic. But Gleneagles is for the very rich, and I was there only as a convalescent, who found it wearisome to walk a full quarter of a mile, from break-fast-room to bedroom and back, for a forgotten hand-kerchief. Great hotels in the Highlands seem to be against nature; at Gleneagles, fortunately, nature has splendour enough to keep even that palatial pile in its place. Besides, it was in October that we stayed there at half-prices, and the excitement of the autumn colours, seen for the first time, made us forget the palm-court and the broad acres of carpet.

As for St Andrews itself, I have visited it on only two occasions, but as a good Darwinian I knew exactly what to expect. Coming back by the railway to the Road Hole, I got into all the troubles, including pitching back from the middle of the road, that Mr Darwin's heroes suffered and overcame; only I suffered and did not over-come. But there is pleasure in mere recognition; and I could well understand how an old friend of mine, a parson, found fulfilment there. A golf-addict, he had been made prisoner by the Turks at Kut, and was led by suffering to vow, in the event of his survival, to take Orders. This he did, unaware that the Trinity he really worshipped was Vardon, Taylor and Braid. He struggled manfully to serve two masters, but in the end succumbed to his ruling passion. Justified by ill-health and capacitated by a legacy, he gave up his cure of souls and retired to St Andrews, where he enjoyed a few years of unalloyed bliss before dying in his sleep.

There is only one drawback to golfing in Scotland: the links are too near to the grouse-moors and the deer-forests. It is exhilarating to find your game improving daily under the eye of a knowing and articulate caddie, who not only sees what is wrong with you but is able, by birthright, to put it into words. But all the time you are teased by memories, of hopes, of deeper satisfactions and greater thrills than golf, even on those delectable links, can afford. Every time you lift your eyes to the distant mountains your heart follows into their recesses, or to the higher tops beyond them, where there are wild things to pursue among surroundings more enchanting still. No mere ball-game can compete, for some of us, with the delights of shooting or stalking; no smooth greens or springy fairways with the heather, the peat-bogs and the high tops. So that, after all, having once been made free of golf in its homeland, of golf at its golfiest, it is perhaps better, for some of us at any rate, to repair to some English links like Brancaster, where no thoughts of grouse or deer will come nibbling at our enjoyment. The Norfolk turf is as firm and close as that of East Lothian; the sea is there, and so are the terns, if not the Solan Geese; and if Tom King the younger was born and bred in Norfolk, his father, old Tom

King, came from Scotland itself, and could be affable
or gruff in the authentic Scots tones. Young Tom had
the lithe figure and the easy swing of the natural golfer,
and liked to walk as fast between shots as I did; for the
sheer game's sake, a round with him was, for me, the
best I have known of golfing: for he set a rhythm which
could, at moments, be faintly caught and followed, and
golf is a game at which example is better than precept.
Could I have afforded to buy Tom King's time in my
younger days, I might possibly have attained to respect-
able mediocrity.

How the indigent young are to fare at golf today,
with a full set of clubs costing seventy pounds, and bags
too heavy to carry, I do not know. Perhaps, except for
the giants who have to compete with the machine-like
American players, the expense and the elaboration will
compel a return to the old methods, when the player,
not the club, was responsible for the length of each shot,
and seven clubs in a light bag were good enough for
those who played golf for the fun of it. And fun it is,
with the added fascination of being the most difficult
game in the world, considering that, unlike all other
games but billiards, you have no opponent to spoil or
thwart your shot. For while to non-golfers it might
well appear that putting is simpler than fiddling, yet
there are thousands of fiddlers playing in orchestras
who would think shame of hitting a wrote note, while
any world-champion at golf will occasionally miss a
short putt.

So let us hope that the fun and the fascination will
induce our grandsons to devise ways of circumventing
the expense, and that they will not allow themselves to
be deprived of yet another of the more vivid enjoy-

ments of leisure. For while few of them may be poets enough to share Mr Darwin's high and heroic approach to the game, they will find on the fairways and greens of our island's links not only fine, striding, active amusement, but the loveliest playgrounds imaginable. Beauty, sought or not, has a way of sinking in, and a game which exposes the players, however indifferent, to its subtle persuasions is not one to be lightly relinquished.

## CHAPTER XVIII

# AN ECCENTRIC IN ITALY

IT must have been in March at latest that the advertisement appeared in the Agony Column of *The Times*. Dorothea Speyer who, being as capable as she is unselfish, makes all the arrangements for our journeys, leaves nothing to chance, and begins her correspondence with Tuscan or Umbrian hotel-keepers at a season when, to most of us, an Italian holiday seems too dreamlike to be real. The advertisement announced that an Italian gentleman (whom I shall call "the Count") was prepared to receive guests, on very reasonable terms, in his Castello. This was situated in a region known to us by repute but as yet unexplored; a countryside full of temptations, of hills and white oxen and vines, within reach of a renowned and ancient city.

The Count's reply was short and businesslike, and our rooms were booked for a date in September. The day came, and it was already dusk when the lordly Italian autobus halted at a tiny hamlet on a main road, ejected our baggage from a cavern in its flank, and left us peering round for the car, or cars, which we had expected to find awaiting us. There was no car; but there was a mule harnessed to two high wheels, between which was slung a kind of cat's cradle of string, and there was a Vespa motor-bicycle, festooned with onions and carrots, leaning against the wall of the post office.

A grey-headed man in his seventies, not undistinguished, limped forward to introduce himself as the Count. We named each other to unreceptive ears: he was not interested in distinguishing between Speyers and Joneses, and did not, I think, grasp that distinction during the whole week we spent under his roof.

"One of the ladies will ride on the Vespa. The others will walk with me."

"And the luggage?"

"The mule will take that."

It did not seem possible that the tangled cat's cradle could support more than one suitcase, but in fact it expanded miraculously until the swollen kitbags and camp-stools of the comfort-loving Joneses, as well as the neat, spare cases of the ascetic Speyers, were swinging together, in one monstrous huddle, between the great wheels.

"But neither of us can ride a motor-bicycle," protested the wives.

"Let me introduce my cook. He will ride the machine; the lady will perch behind him."

A slim figure advanced, and we all shook hands with the cook, to whom, in the next few days, we were to owe so much.

The lot fell upon my wife; unable, on account of the dangling vegetables, to bestride the pillion-seat, she sat side-saddle, precariously balanced, with her arms round the cook's waist. The Vespa roared away into the darkness. I did not like it at all.

It was a mile and a half to the Castello; a mile along the tarmac, and half a mile climbing up through the vineyards by a footpath that broke, here and there, into flights of stairs.

The Count had but recently recovered from a broken leg, and his pace was one mile an hour. Accordingly it took us one and a half hours to reach our destination. For normal legs a mile an hour is not an easy pace. It requires constant mental effort to achieve this tempo. Not only must each stride be shortened, but the motion of the limbs through the air must be slowed down. We arrived exhausted by lack of effort.

But to our host this snail-like progression was an opportunity, not a drawback. He had a great deal to tell us, and in that preliminary crawl he was able to get through the prologue of an unfinished monologue which lasted a week. His theme was himself, and a good theme too, had there been less of it; never dull, sometimes credible, and developed, day by day, with a disarming certainty that no other subject could conceivably be more enthralling to his listeners. Darkness is a useful ally to a talker out of doors; we had nothing to watch but our steps; and by the time we arrived at the lighted doorway of the Castello, crowded with the welcoming faces of his staff, we had lived with our host through his English public school and college, his thirty years as an Indian Civil Servant, his clashes with Curzon, his decisive influence on Indian affairs as *eminence grise* to Gandhi on the one side and to a series of viceroys on the other. Why his English should be faultless and idiomatic was never clear to us; his status as a titled Italian landowner, although visible to the eye, was less easy to square with his long service to the British Crown. We always intended to ask him about this, but there was never a gap in his talk wide enough for the putting of a question, and after a week under his roof we had still not solved the mystery of an Italian citizen (as he certainly was) serving in the I.C.S.

The Castello was large, four-square, and pink, with a turret at one corner to justify its name, and that slight outward thrust of the foot of each corner as it feels for the ground, which gives a fortress-like air to so many Italian farmsteads. Its rooms were lofty and full of dignity; the long dining-room had a barrel roof, arabesqued in fresco; the views from the bedroom windows, framed between white walls, were of the same hillsides, coloured like a honeycomb and dotted with bushes of mulberry or maple, that are to be seen in Piero della Francesca's backgrounds.

There were other English guests, pleasant people with whom we never got acquainted, since they spent their days on long motor expeditions, and in the evenings, when we all met in the long dining-room, the Count's monologue from the head of the table allowed for no private conversation. One other figure was present at meals, and only at meals—that of the melancholy, speechless Contessa, knowing no word of English, hating the countryside, dreaming of her beloved Rome, and unappeased, to her husband's perennial indignation and surprise, by the chic apartments, all yellow satin and bows, which he had provided to solace her for a solitary and loveless existence. "She adores me," he told my wife, sauntering among the vines with husband on one side and wife on the other. He even complied with a demand that he should repeat this in Italian to the Contessa, to provoke a sudden outburst of fury from the unhappy lady in which my wife could only recognise the word "egoismo" a dozen times repeated.

At our first dinner, where the food was delicious and

the home-made red wine plentiful and pleasing, the
Count, having sketched his career on the road, described to us his present way of living. The most striking
thing about it was that he never went to bed. He sat up
all night in his library, typing out his nightly letter to
his daughter, composing poetry, or working at his
*magnum opus*, an English-Italian dictionary. At three
o'clock he had a light meal; at four he went to his bath
and slept in it until the water became chilly enough to
wake him. He then dried and dressed and went back
to his typewriter. A doze in his chair before dinner
was the only other repose he allowed himself.

The roomy house had an admirable *confort moderne*,
but only one, for guests of both sexes. The only means
of reaching it lay through our host's library. Here he
sat like a spider in the centre of its web, waiting for his
victims to come to him, as come, sooner or later, they
must. Access to the place was uninterrupted, for he
recognised a purposeful gait in his stream of visitors,
but on the return journey he pounced. "Just read this,"
he would say, handing his reluctant guest a copy of the
nocturnal letter to his daughter. This daughter was a
nun, a member of an enclosed order; but she was also
an architect, responsible for the building operations of
her order in all parts of the world. But the letters did
not touch her profession; they were uniformly concerned with the Roman Catholic religion, which he
attacked and ridiculed with undeniable power and
resource. It is hardly credible that a busy woman should
have opened and read three hundred and sixty-five
assaults on all she held most dear every year of her life;
he admitted that she made no reply to them. His
motive, he said, was his devotion to her, and his care

for her eternal welfare. But it was clear that he craved for certainty that somebody, no matter who, should read and admire these pugnacious missives.

By the end of the first dinner we had learned that we must be seen and not heard, for there had been a tone of shocked surprise in his voice as he exclaimed to his neighbour, when I turned to murmur some polite nothings to my own: "That man keeps talking!" At subsequent meals our host made far more intimate and interesting disclosures than those about his bathing, sleeping and writing habits. He broke to us, albeit with perfect casualness, that he had been reincarnated many times, and could recollect much of his former lives. He had been, for instance, Erasmus. This, as a beginning, was impressive enough; yet he was not as lucky in his audience as he might have been. For by a coincidence I had been lately re-reading Froude's *Life and Letters of Erasmus*, and was able to check his recollections by some of the great man's recorded words. They by no means always agreed; and the Count grew a little restive on hearing that he had done this or that on a visit to England in the sixteenth century. He could hardly deny his own letters, yet was reluctant to admit that his memory might be at fault. But the plain fact was that he had clearly forgotten, among other things, his visit to Walsingham.

We did not hear much more of Erasmus, but there were startling revelations to come. He was strong on the Higher Criticism, a subject in which I too have always been interested, but it was slightly disconcerting, at the dinner-table, to hear a discourse on the authorship of the Fourth Gospel abruptly closed with: "And I ought to know, as I wrote it myself." He had also been

John the Disciple, and had lively recollections of the Last Supper, but it was not as that John, but in a later incarnation, that he wrote the Gospel. There were other incarnations which I have forgotten, all announced with perfect matter-of-factness, and without any air of wishing to astonish.

And yet he was genuinely well read, and had an acute as well as a well-stocked mind. In his sustained attack on his daughter's Church he relied on rational argument, not on his dinner-table claims to first-hand knowledge. And he knew his texts. At the end of dinner we dispersed, early as it was, to our own rooms, for the formal drawing-room had neither armchairs nor reading-lamps, and the comfortable living-room in which we foregathered before meals was at that hour sacred to the staff. There were plenty of servants, both young men and girls, friendly and efficient, and it was our host's custom, after dinner, to sit among them in his big armchair, while they ranged themselves on sofas and looked at the English illustrated weeklies, such as the *Illustrated London News*, the *Sphere* and the *Tatler*. It was a patriarchal scene, and the perfect ease of the servants in his presence was a tribute to his innate civility. We noticed the same good feeling and friendliness between the Count and his share-cropping tenants, whose farms, where silkworms were cultivated as well as vines, olives and maize, were a pleasure to look at. The white oxen or heifers were already ploughing the yellowish clay between the rows of pollarded maple or mulberry from which the vines sagged, the beasts groomed and sleek, the land made use of to the last square foot. There was an air of prosperity and contentment everywhere.

One of the Count's activities, in spite of his being
dead-lame and in his middle seventies, was lawn-tennis.
"I have never lost a game of tennis in my life," he told
us; and was not afraid, for all his boasting, to let us
watch him in action, for he had an excellent hard court,
on which he played a set or two each evening with his
servants, or with young men who roared up the hill
on Vespas from the neighbouring town. And it must
be said that, although the standard of play was moderate,
we did not see the old boy beaten. Did his grateful
opponents pull their punches? It is possible, but if so it
was cleverly done.

Good food and wine, charming rooms, excellent
service, a countryside with every delight that makes the
thought of Italy so warming in black English Januaries,
what more could the traveller want? Had we, like our
fellow-guests, been able to use the Castello merely for
dining and sleeping, it would have been a place to
revisit again and again. But we were not able. There
were walks, and there was the neighbouring town,
compact with beauties; but the elderly traveller without
a car is tethered by a short rope, and must be always
homing. And there sat the spider. There was no escape.

The letters and the poems must be read and admired,
the everlasting saga of self must be listened to. It was
too much.

At dinner on the last evening a worm turned. The
Count, at the other end of the table, was discoursing
on his own character. "Never in my life," he exclaimed,
with a glance at his patient wife gazing blankly into
space, "have I known what it is to be in love."

"That," I said loudly, "is untrue."

"What do you mean, untrue?"

"You have been in love with yourself all your life."

He was actually, for a second or two, taken aback; then recovered, to give us proofs of his modesty and selflessness.

It was rude of me, to my host at his own table. Luckily I have little doubt but that he imputed the bad manners to "that fellow Speyer." For we left him, after a week under his roof, as anonymously as we arrived. Not once had he enquired as to our origins, our professions, our interests, our homes, or any single thing about us. We were an audience, and that was sufficient.

All the same, had there been a lavatory on the ground floor I believe we should have returned. There was, at times, good fun to be had from such fanatical egoism. What was not tolerable was being button-holed through inescapable necessity.

## CHAPTER XIX

# VINEGAR

A MOST distinguished critic, who is also a friend, has told me that what he found lacking in my first two volumes of memories was "vinegar." Nobody, he pointed out, can have lived so contentedly as I have pretended to do, with so much to enjoy, so little to dislike. I saw his point, for few can relish "vinegar" in other people's books more keenly than do I; but on reflection I concluded that the lack of 'bite' in my reminiscences was mainly due (apart from the law of libel) to some quirk of nature, common to most of us, whereby we forget our hates but remember our loves. All summers were fine in our youth, all Christmases clear and frosty; we forget the enemies feared or hated at school or college, the friends who betrayed or dropped us, the heartaches and failure, the dullness of routine, the recurrent dreariness of a thousand Mondays. A few can be recalled by an effort, but most are comfortably buried beneath the rich soil of our satisfactions.

My third volume was described by one reader, in a letter to another who, although a stranger, felt it his duty to pass it on, as: "nasty, cruel, malicious, and in the worst possible taste." That ought perhaps to have put me right with myself over this question of vinegar, but it did not. Instead, I was much troubled and perturbed. *Sauce piquante* is one thing; cruelty and malice quite another. However, being put on my mettle, I have searched my memory for things which have been hateful, or at any rate distasteful or embarrassing, to me. For I am not sure that embarrassment, even when due to my own shortcomings, does not excite as much resentment as an injury. One of my earlier *bêtes-noires* was Mrs Letitia Barbauld. I should have been glad to see her lie dead at my feet; yet her only offence was to have written a book called *Hymns in Prose*. These hymns embarrassed me, at the age of six, very much, and it was some years before I understood that "prose" was not necessarily what Mrs Barbauld wrote. It was a "Sunday book," in itself a handicap to any author, and it was bound in a sort of dirty green, very lowering to the spirits. And who but the writer of such stuff would be called Barbauld? The next author to offend me was a very great man indeed, none other than Charles Dickens, but curiously enough I do not remember visiting my resentment for the embarrassment he caused me upon Dickens himself, but upon those people who, unlike myself, thought the Fat Boy in Pickwick funny. Nobody likes to be found short of a sense of humour, and my grudge was against those who told me I ought to laugh as they did at that grievous Fat Boy. Dickens was acquitted, because he had made the others laugh; it was their guffaws that embarrassed me. It was the same with Mr Alfred Jingle, that human machine-gun, whose staccato sputterings bored me to tears; it was the pro-Jingles, not his creator, whom I resented. I can only hope that the Beaumont schoolboy with whom I lately quarrelled over the incomparable Mr Micawber, in whom he finds nothing but dreariness, likewise holds me, and not Dickens, to be at fault.

I have all my life been at enmity with Mary Queen of Scots. I believe this arose, in the first place, from sheer disappointment with her looks. Quite early I came across a reproduction of some contemporary portrait of this reputed beauty which shocked me to the core. It was long before I learnt that she had blown up a husband with gunpowder—a feat for which I might have easily forgiven a truly beautiful woman; it was the hard horse-face that revolted me. I felt I had been badly let down, and could never again take an interest in her. Maturer knowledge of her character and career has done nothing to make a reconciliation between us possible. Mary Queen of Scots and I remain at arm's length.

Not that I am incapable of forgiveness. The most bitter feelings I can recall were directed against Baldwin during his last administration. The extremes of animosity come from a sense of impotence; so long as it lies within one's power to take some action, to make an effective protest, hostility can be wholehearted without hatred or even personal dislike. It is impotence that makes us writhe, and writhing that leads to bitterness. As a private individual I had to stand by and watch a Prime Minister, supported by an enormous Parliamentary majority and most of my personal friends, continue to neglect the defences of the Empire in the face of no remote possibility, but of an open and deadly threat, of attack. There were moments, I believe, when I felt almost less indignation against the Teutonic Wolf who, after all, was acting according to his bestial nature, than against the British Shepherd who would take no precautions to safeguard his fold. With our very life as a nation at stake, Mr Baldwin's personal charm, goodness and idealism went for nothing: they were all irrelevant to the kind of leadership our predicament required.

On Baldwin's retirement I re-directed my enmity towards Chamberlain. But with a difference. For I realised that Chamberlain had inherited, as Whig noblemen inherited the gout, a weakness for which he was not personally responsible, and that any Minister, a Churchill himself, would have been compelled to play for time (as indeed Churchill was compelled in the case of the Burma Road). Chamberlain's offence was not so much his policy, forced upon him by our woeful lack of armaments, as his obtuseness and vanity. His persistence in believing himself capable, despite all the evidence, of bringing Hitler to see reason; his credulity over "peace in our time"; his vanity in dispensing with advice and ignoring intelligence which did not suit him; these were the things that aroused the baffled fury of his opponents. It was fortunate for Chamberlain that we had no inkling, until after the war, that he had submitted to Mussolini for approval the draft of a speech he proposed to make in the House of Commons. Had that leaked out, he would have been swept away.

The peculiarity about my anger against these two Prime Ministers is that it was aimed at two admirable men, and, in Baldwin's case, a most attractive one. Both had honesty, public spirit and goodwill in the highest degree. The years have passed; I have read their lives; I have found much to respect, even to admire, in both of them. They bore great burdens; they had courage and character. Their misfortune was to be raised, by our political system, to a height far beyond their capacities, and not to know it. The dangers that beset them were tremendous and unprecedented, and they were no

match for them. How many of their predecessors would
have been a match? Chatham? Perhaps. Pitt? Doubtful.
Disraeli? We have no evidence: he was never tried in
the fullness of his powers. Lloyd-George? Possibly.
But for the rest, if you go back two hundred years,
can you name a Prime Minister whom you could
confidently back to have so conducted our affairs after
1933 as to have prevented the Second World War?
Such reflections make an end of all personal animus. It
is not a man's own fault that he finds himself in a
situation far beyond his powers.

Apart from these two statesmen, the late Mrs
Barbauld and Mary Queen of Scots, I can recall no
personal hatreds, although no doubt I have had many
temporary and fugitive resentments against individuals.
(Execration of Nazis, Fascists, and all atrocity-mongers
does not count; it is shared by us all. And there is not
the same sense of writhing impotence; to play a part,
however exiguous, in righteous wars helps to sweat the
poison of hatred out of one's system.) But I have
many dislikes and prejudices—some of them directed
against the most praiseworthy objects, to which
admirable people devote their energies.

P.E.N., for instance. I am a member of P.E.N., having been ordered to become one by an authoress whose
charm and beauty made refusal out of the question. But
I have never been able to understand why writers, even
those who speak and write the same language, should
want to get together. The Society of Authors, yes—for
that is a purely business affair for the practical purpose
of watching over the members' pockets. In questions
of copyright, of royalties and so on, a lone author
needs protection in a world of wild publishers,

theatre-managers, and B.B.C.'s. But the members of the
Society of Authors, other than their elected committee
who watch over them, do not meet, let alone in Zürich,
to talk about themselves. They pay their subscription,
sit at home and, it is to be supposed, get on with their
writing. But P.E.N.'s whole purpose is to get authors
(and the more foreign they are, the better) to meet
together (and the further from England, the better)
for discussions and worse. (By worse I mean such things
as poetry-readings. There are a handful of highly-
trained actors and actresses whose speaking of verse can
enhance its beauty or power to move. But they are rare
and expensive. People untrained in elocution, and that
includes most authors, only give pain; to an audience
that knows a poem, and has heard it with the inward ear,
any recital of it by a speaker not in the John Gielgud
class is unacceptable.) Now, unless the whole point of
P.E.N. is to enable a few writers to have a free jaunt
abroad and to see Ankara, or Tokyo, or wherever it is,
what is gained by the personal contact of writer with
writer? I have no doubt that Sir Oswald Sitwell and
Mr. P. G. Wodehouse enjoy each other's company,
whether or not they have read each other's books, but
why should I pay a guinea a year to bring about their
encounter? Will it have the faintest effect on the style
or matter of either in his next book? It is what a writer
puts into his work that should interest another writer,
not what he says over a cocktail, or even declaims,
through an interpreter, from a tribune. If the time
devoted to travel and discussion was given instead to
reading foreign authors, it would be more profitably
spent. And my guinea, too, would be saved; to buy,
perhaps, a copy of *Dr Zhivago*. Birds of a feather flock

together, but are writers birds of a feather? The more original, the more creative, a mind, the more it will need, in this clamorous world, solitude and *recueillement*, not conferences and cocktails. Besides, there is always the danger that a personal meeting may lead to disillusion. Not all authors are like the late Max Beerbohm, whose personality was on a level with his best work. And it is difficult, on returning to a favourite book, not to be haunted by memories of some small vanities, the down-drawn corners of a mouth, the gush or gaucheries of its author seen in the flesh. No, as I see it—and I am in a hopeless minority—there is no bond between writers as such that requires expression by personal intercourse. I would rather that each should warm his five wits alone, like the owl, and say what he has to say with his pen, not his mouth.

I have mentioned cocktails. Cocktail-parties arouse in me a feeling of repulsion amounting to venom. It is not merely that, being six foot four in height, I can only see the tops of women's hats, and hear with difficulty the sweet nothings that are uttered from below them, nor because of the fatigue, akin to that felt in a geological museum, which overpowers me. It is that I can never think of anything to say, and my neighbours never say anything to make me think. The truth is that we are all unhappy together. Nobody really enjoys noise and chatter and heat. Besides, if once in a way I encounter a friend who has something to say, I am dragged away, before he has time to say it, to stand tongue-tied in front of an Ambassadress with wandering eyes. At each party I add to the number of people whom I shall offend, by forgetting their faces, at the next, and cut, unaware, those met at the one before.

Cocktail-parties debase social intercourse, spoil our dinners, and diminish goodwill towards men. They ought to be abolished by common consent.

A more idiosyncratic dislike of mine is for pageants and most forms of dressing-up. I am on the side of the draggled player, sheltering among the laurels, who when asked by the pageant-master: "Are you Appius Claudius?" replied: "No, miserable as be-damned." It is not that I have no appreciation of magnificence. Had I been stone-deaf, I could have sat happily through Benjamin Britten's *Gloriana* merely to gaze in delighted wonder at John Piper's scenery. On the stage, at Glyndebourne, in a Roman Basilica, backgrounds, costumes or vestments cannot be too gorgeous for me. But there they are in their proper places, functional and to the point, since they are ancillary to the main business, which is acting, music or liturgy. But pageants are almost always affairs of dressing-up for its own sake; the "book" is depressingly dull, the performers can rarely act or speak, the historical incidents carry no conviction of verisimilitude. The Joint-Master of Hounds as Joan of Arc and the bank manager as Dunois are not even comic.

Peers in their robes are a distressing spectacle. The close-cropped modern head peeping over the top of the ermine, with bows and ribbons adding an air of babyhood, is a sad sight. At the least a wig like Marlborough's should be worn to counterbalance the cumbersome bulk of the robes and caps. Besides, a moustache, for some reason I cannot fathom, makes all fancy dress absurd. A Knight of the Garter is all right, if he has a leg, for his jaunty hat and feather give him height and presence. Even so, I prefer the greatest of them all in his siren-suit. He is *plus chez soi.*

I am inconsistent enough to except the case of judges and barristers. If I am to be hanged, I prefer to be sentenced by a judge in a full-bottomed wig, after being defended by a barrister in a curly one. The barrister appears more learned, the judge more judicial, than do those waistcoatless judges and lawyers one sees in American films, where the judge is indistinguishable from the juryman, the lawyer from the usher. But here again a moustache is fatal. I am also wholeheartedly for the Guards, Foot or Horse. But their gorgeous apparel is native to them, like his feathers to a peacock; I cannot, when I see them march, believe that they ever shed their glory; I picture them lying down at night in rows, like the toy soldiers I ranged so carefully in their boxes as a boy.

To balance my dislike of dressing-up, I also disapprove of dressing-down. It was well enough for Shelley and Byron to wear turn-down collars over their coats, without neckties, but they were poets: our modern slovens are not. The worst case of dressing-down, however, is that of the clergy. Here are dedicated men, set apart to preach "Good News," a gospel of hope, not despair, who depress our spirits at every sight of them. Ought not the Prince of Peace to have his servants as gloriously arrayed as the devotees of the God of War? Not that I recommend bearskins and gold lace; a poor curate's salary, even a bishop's, would not run to it. But at least they might wear grey tweeds or flannels, and a coloured tie; uniforms, but with a cheerful, even gay impact upon the beholders. As it is, their rusty black clothes and near-white dog-collars belie their message. Why should the presence of a clergyman lower the temperature of any gathering? Why must

they so often be over-hearty, if not to counteract the
gloom induced by their dismal costumes? If soldiers
and sailors were dressed as clergymen, would you get
a single recruit? It is bad enough to be handicapped by
dogma; at least our clergy might be spared the dog-
collar.

The thought of these laborious underpaid men
reminds me of another drawback which not all, but
some of them, suffer, and one which I find curiously
repellent. I mean the ecclesiastical intonation, the
peculiar pronunciation, never used by laymen. To have
heard it in its extreme form you must have attended
weddings in a certain church in Mayfair, where it had
developed into a whine which made the service almost
unintelligible to a lay ear. (At the wedding-party afterwards the speaker, curiously enough, talked like everybody else, proving that the whine was "laid on" for the
occasion.) But it is fairly prevalent in a milder form. In a
village where my Yeomanry was billeted before embarking for France there was an amiable curate called
Mr Snooks. Mr Snooks used to bicycle, morning and
evening, past the window of our Mess. We used to
shout, "Good morning, Mr Snooks," and "Good-night,
Mr Snooks," for the pleasure of hearing his "Güd
merning, Güd merning," and "Güd nate, Güd nate."
When I asked Mr Snooks how much I should tip the
charlady who swept the schoolroom after a machine-
gun lesson, he replied, "Aynything you lake, aynything
you lake, but not mower than sixpence." (This odd
trick of making a disyllable out of 'more' was repeated
by a padre at the Cavalry machine-gun school who,
when offered a glass of sherry by a neighbouring squire,
rebuked his kindly host with a severe, "Nert in woah-

time".) I was assured by another padre who shared our
Mess in France that this strange pronunciation was not
due, like the nasal voices of the seventeenth-century
Puritans, to holiness, but to a reason I had not guessed.
This padre habitually pronounced "Yes" and "No" as
"Yerse" and "Nö", and, at church parade, the word
"Knowledge" as if it were two words "Know" and
"ledge," instead of the usual "knolledge." One evening,
after a second glass of port, I was emboldened to ask
him why he made these eccentric noises. He was most
good-natured about it. He had been taught them, he
explained, at a theological college, not because the
noises were in any way supposed to indicate piety in
the speaker, but because the ordinands were drawn
from so many regions, and spoke with such diverse
accents, that it was thought necessary to put them
through a severe course of elocution. They were made
to imitate their teacher until his pronunciation became
second nature in them, and the teacher just happened to
be a man who said "Yerse" and all the rest. There was,
he assured me, nothing more to it than that. But had
the machine-gun padre been at this theological college?
Had Mr Snooks? And the Mayfair vicar? I do not know.
But bearing in mind the Cromwellian spoil-sports (did
some of them take with them to Massachusets the seed
of the Yankee twang?), I find it hard to believe that the
accent of the teacher of elocution was natural in him,
and had nothing to do with his profession.

How hard it is to be sincere! In reading over the fore-
going paragraphs I find that I wrote of this trick of
speech as being "repellent": in fact, as my story of Mr
Snooks proves, it has been a pleasure and an amusement
to me. It feeds, in an unworthy way, my anti-clericalism

and supplies ammunition to my love of mimicry. I experience a collector's glow when I come across a fresh instance of it. It should have no place in a chapter about my dislikes. But then how rarely, in finding fault, do we admit, even to ourselves, the fun we get out of doing so.

A confessed anti-clerical ought, it may be thought, to justify, when discussing his antipathies, one so serious and revealing. But I have already done so in two books, *Beyond Belief* and *The Bishop and the Cobbler*; besides, my anti-clericalism is impersonal and without venom. It is based on moral and metaphysical grounds. I would defend it to the last gasp. Here I am exposing my prejudices, often irrational, for the reader to deride or to compare with his own.

A prejudice shared, so far as I know, by none but which amounts with me almost to abhorrence, is against the headdress of women out hunting. A woman in a top-hat or bowler hat, with her hair squeezed into a tight bun behind, revolts me. I have never been able to believe the tales told of loose sexual morals in smart hunting sets, because it seems to me that one glance at a lady at a Meet must extinguish desire, or romance, once and for all. Where the crusader, before embarking, locked his wife in the belt of chastity, I believe the fox-hunter, before taking a day off for the Cheltenham races, should gum to her head the hard hat and bun. They would be, in my view, an inviolable protection of virtue. I suppose hunting women would plead that they were entitled to be safeguarded against concussion. Then let them wear the less unbecoming hunting-cap, but with locks flowing free. Better still, let them put sex before self, take risks, and go riding, as did their

ancestors, in velvet hat and feathers, with a jabot of lace
and embroidered gauntlets. Or would that wreck too
many homes in Leicestershire?

Women in trousers, except the very young and slim,
are another trial I find hard to bear. I sympathise with
them for wanting to share our masculine leg-room, but
the wisdom of all ages and climates has recognised
certain fundamental truths about the female figure, and
has draped it below the waist. One can respect the
trousered woman's lack of vanity, without being able
to enjoy its consequences.

As for hair worn to look like a horse's tail, I imagine
all men dislike it as much as I do. I can only hope it
brings its own punishment, in the form of "disgrace in
men's eyes."

Ballet-skirts are a private abomination of my own.
They bisect the female thigh, and a repellently muscular
one at that, at a most ill-chosen level. Nature has refused
beautiful knees to most women, and the act of dancing
on the tips of the toes distorts even a shapely leg.
Pavlova in *Carnaval* was a poem, for she wore drapery
in which to dance. But in the traditional ballet-skirts,
even that beautiful creature failed to charm me. It is
interesting to speculate upon how many millions of
pounds spent on diamonds and champagne, on horses
and carriages and sables, might have been saved in the
nineteenth century had the Kings and Princes and
bankers of that prosperous era shared in this antipathy
of mine. But they did not, any more than did Degas,
who was seduced (as were so many of their wearers)
by these odious little skirts.

I cannot bear shopping. I do not mind dropping into
a tobacconist's shop, or even a chemist's, for there is

no choice to be made there, no occasion for hesitations, no exposure to salesmanship by the person who serves me. I can order a pair of shoes with equanimity, since the bootmaker has my last and a couple of words suffice. But to buy ties, or socks, or underclothes is a penance. I am embarrassed by the very existence of shop-walkers and male assistants, having a feeling that men are unmanned by such occupations. I can never persuade them that if I ask for a dark blue tie with white spots, it is useless to show me green ties with yellow zigzags, or that because things are "being worn" they shall not be worn by me. I have no idea "what size" I take in long pants, and resent the look of patient pity with which they visit my ignorance. I hate to see neat parcels undone which, because of my abnormal length, will have to be done up again. I find it impossible to believe that things I bought in my youth at 7/6d are now 84/6d, and am apt to accuse these hardworked underlings of profiteering. When the shop-walker tells me, "You want the haberdashery," I contradict him, since, never having discovered what haberdashery is, it is obvious that I cannot want it. I am equally peevish when informed that I want "hose."

These irritations are no doubt shared by every male person, and would not be worth mentioning but for the light they throw on the difference between the sexes. For most women enjoy a bout of shopping. It might seem a harmless enough amusement for them; unfortunately, there is a sinister side to it. For women out shopping, unlike men, allow their pleasure to swamp their humanity. They do not care how many neat parcels are untied for them in vain. They have no mercy or consideration for those behind them in a queue. A man, if there be only one other customer behind him, will take a pair of grey socks instead of the blue he prefers rather than keep that customer waiting. A woman will slowly turn over twenty herrings, all the same shape and size, before picking one for her shopping bag. I have even known a woman treat a ticket-office as a shop and, with half a dozen fellow-travellers behind her, enjoy a long conversation with the head and shoulders of the booking-clerk about the place to which she was going and the reasons for her journey. She would, I feel sure, have liked a dozen tickets to be spread out for her to choose from.

I am an enemy of gambling: not on moral grounds but because, having no taste for it whatever, I find the amount of space devoted to it in the papers tiresome. On Saturdays especially I have to turn over many pages of football results in search of, let us say, some vital news from the Middle East. The racing news and Stock Exchange prices have always occupied their accustomed pages and cause no trouble; but since the craze for the pools came in, association football, in some form or other, is apt to break out all over the newspaper. Photographs of players and managers, heavy headlines about transfer fees, tables and coupons and all the complicated apparatus for enriching the pools' promoters surround, like a viscous Sargasso sea, a few islands of news. That I cannot share the ruling passion of so many of my fellow-countrymen must be put down, I suspect, to a "complex" dating from early childhood. Money was then so scarce and so precious that the idea of losing a sixpence and getting nothing in return was a dreadful one. To this day I regard with astonishment the light-hearted way my fellow-members

of the club pay their pounds and enter their names in a
great ruled sheet of cardboard headed "Derby Sweep-
stake." Don't they realise the weight of the odds against
them? And that their pound is almost certainly gone
for good? It would be pleasant to win, I admit; but I
find it impossible to believe that I might draw a horse,
let alone the winner. It is not the sort of thing that
happens to me. I am compelled, on occasions, as at
charity balls and church fêtes, to go in for raffles. I have
once, and only once, won a prize. I won it by the sheer
weight of my investment. It was a little wooden paper-
knife. I have played roulette at Monte Carlo, and with
great daring placed my five francs on red, which has
an even chance of turning up. Black, of course, turned
up, and the croupier, inured to human suffering,
stretched out his long rake and collared my stake without a pitying glance in my direction. My wife, who
loves a flutter, and like other votaries of Fortune is
rewarded by an occasional smile, turned one *louis d'or*
into thirty-six with a run of reds. We needed a service-
lift: one more red, and it would be ours. Should she
venture? Unluckily I whispered, "Yes." My inter-
ference was enough: black turned up. It took two scrapes
of the rake to remove her winnings—half a service-lift
went with them. She left the room amused and
exhilarated at having been within one turn of her
heart's desire. I left it thinking gloomily of how much
we could have done with that *louis d'or*. Decidedly I am
not a gambler.

Another quite unreasonable prejudice of mine is
against motor-cars. I have made the same use of them as
everybody else; they have enormously increased the
sum of my enjoyments. But I cannot take to them for

their own sake. For one thing, I am irritated at being unable to tell one make from another. In the days when I owned cars, if I attended a point-to-point, or an agricultural show, or Henley Regatta, or any place where cars are parked in rows, I had to tie a handkerchief to the bonnet of my own car so that I should be able to recognise it. I could not even memorise the letters and figures on the number-plate. Then again, I am bored almost to despair by talk about cars. I have stayed in a country house for shooting where the men discussed cars over the port, in the smoking-room, on the way to the covers, for three days without a let-up. Their knowledge was extraordinary; but what is there, in a machine used for getting us from place to place, to talk about? We do not discuss knives, or spoons, or boots, or sewing-machines—all more necessary to our comfort and convenience than cars. We do not even discuss legs, which, if means of transport are a fit topic at all, should surely come before cars? If no man would willingly exchange his legs for a car, then let legs, not cars, come first to be argued about.

Breaking speed-records, on land, or on the water, is an activity I watch with a cold and hostile eye. Speed in the air, alas, is a matter of defence and must be encouraged; but the speeds achieved by Bluebird or racing cars, at chosen moments of calm on a lake, or on built-up racing-tracks, has no significance even for modern war. To make it a matter of national prestige is journalistic nonsense. I respect the nerve and skill of the men who break, sometimes records, sometimes their necks; but too many things already move too fast for comfort these days, and I wish they would put their gifts to some better use. At the other end of the scale,

I suppose it to be arguable that it is silly to care whether a human being can run a mile in under four minutes. For even so he is not only ridiculously slow compared with other animals, but so little faster than the over-four-minutes runner as to make no practical difference. Can any thoughtful person really applaud these milers? I find myself doing so. True, I still think of them all as called Roger Bannister, because I used to watch him, year by year, when he ran for Oxford. The ease and grace of his motions, and that amazing sprint when, half-way round the last lap, his stride lengthened and quickened and the gap between himself and his opponents became wider and wider, never failed to excite and exhilarate me. A great athlete has more than physical beauty; his limbs are obedient to high courage and a conqueror's will. Talk about a Bannister's legs could never be dull; it would touch upon art and the human spirit.

I have a profound aversion to committees and board meetings. For one thing, they are bound up with the dreariest of all sights—a long table with neither food nor drink set out upon it—only paper, pencils and blotting-paper. Such a table re-inflicts upon me those pangs of my infancy, suffered, as I have told, when, peeping from the night-nursery, I found the day-nursery table not, as I had hoped, covered with a white cloth and dishes, but still draped in dull red checks. Dullness always gets me down, and nothing is duller than a board room.

And what a way of doing business! A committee of three, with myself as chairman, might be tolerable; we could sit in armchairs, with coffee between us, and talk at our ease, with quick despatch. But at board meetings

I never was chairman; there was no coffee; people began, "Er—," and went on with "actually," or "as a matter of fact"; they rambled, they doodled, they shook their heads when I spoke. It was all very depressing. Men who are sharp and clear in their own offices become vague and generalising in a board room. Are they all a little afraid of each other, or is it simply that the clean pink blotting-paper sucks up their thoughts? Out in the street their heads grow clear again; they tell each other, crisply, what ought to have been done. I have known weighty decisions taken in the office lavatory, but rarely, if ever, round a table. There the only quick decision is to take the minutes as read, not so much, I suspect, because we remember our last month's deliberations as because we prefer not to be reminded of them. I believe the real work of all companies to be done between board meetings, and that those depressing affairs could be abolished with no shareholder a penny the worse.

The truth is, I suppose, that committees and boards are intended, not to get things done, but to spread responsibility in case of miscarriages. But where the responsibility lies, there it should be borne. The doodlers at the other end of the table who have not understood, or who have objected and been overruled, or have had no opinion to give, are not really fair game. And they ought never to have been there.

Board meetings remind me of bawdiness, not for phonetic reasons, but because they occasionally begin, or end, with the latest Stock Exchange joke. I enjoy bawdiness, like the majority of men and women, because, humour being largely a sense of the incongruous, sex, so magnificent, almost godlike, in its gifts, so niggling in its mechanism, cannot help being often ludicrous. If bishops are never amused by it, President Lincoln never failed to be; and the tradition of honest bawdy, from the Greeks through Shakespeare to the Stock Exchange, is not one to be ashamed of.

But though far from being a Puritan, I cannot stomach the word "dirty" applied to bawdy stories. Some such stories really are dirty, and I find them revolting. But in our own hygienic society, with cleanliness the rule, there is no excuse for applying the word "dirty" to amusing anecdotes about the predica-ments, the absurdities, which result from the strongest human passion being dependent, for its full expression, upon a preposterous and penny-wise apparatus. (It is, incidentally, astonishing to me how the late Pope, Pius XII, could have brought himself, in his Encyclical letter *Humani Generis*, to press upon his flock the duty of believing the story of Adam and Eve, as told in Genesis. One can understand the slow evolution of our deplorable economical arrangements for reproduction, but that an Omnipotent God, with a Divine imagination, should have created such organs as the best He could do is really beyond belief.)

No, "dirty" stories should be absolutely barred even in smoking-rooms, and funny stories about sex should never be confused with them. And I do not think I am alone in thinking that even legitimate bawdy should be talked only in intimate gatherings of persons sharing a common background. In theatres or music-halls, jokes about sex can be embarrassing. They should never be overheard by the man or maid who hands you the potatoes, nor exchanged with strangers. For, in spite of their common repute, bawdy jokes are delicate things that need careful handling; otherwise they are liable to explode at the wrong moment, or to misfire. And since honest laughter, and never sniggering, is their *raison d'être*, they may be relayed only to those who are capable of it.

From sex to politicians may seem a long jump to take, but for me there is a link, since one of my grievances against professional politicians of all parties is their refusal to put first things first. And one of those first things, in the world today, seems, to me at any rate, to be the question of birth-control. A Welfare State that is prepared to look after every living person from cradle to grave, but has no concern for the number or the quality of its protégés, is surely an absurdity. Such a State is in the position of an innkeeper who attempts to provide beds and food without knowing how many guests are to be expected. It is common sense that the size and resources of a country can support a population of so many and no more, and that the quality of citizens, physical and mental, is of the first importance. Yet no politician, or even statesman, that I know of (except possibly Mr Nehru) has ever put the control of procreation on his list of priorities. In the long run, neglect of the problem could lead to the collapse of civilisation, or, at the best, the end of any form of democratic government. For if you rule by counting heads, and the heads become so numerous, so unkempt, and so thick, that the majority of them will be unable to take a sensible decision on any subject, you must obviously revert to authoritarian government or dissolve in helpless anarchy. Of all human responsibilities, the begetting of children should be one of those to be taken most seriously, with forethought and concern for the child's

future, as well as for society at large. In fact, there is
no human activity more haphazard, improvident and
ill-regulated. In Catholic countries, what ought to be
preached in all churches as a solemn duty, is regarded as
a sin, and condemned out of hand. There is talk of a
natural law which forbids the use of contraceptives. But
hair grows by a natural law, and even Catholic priests
shave their faces and even the tops of their heads. The
truth is, of course, that men are checking, obstructing
and upsetting natural laws every time they pump water
uphill, build dams, harness rivers or control the forces
of nature in any manner. To allow the physically and
mentally degenerate to reproduce themselves at will is
a crime against society, a betrayal of the dignity of Man.
In non-Catholic western countries educated people
today are in fact regulating their families; the ignorant
are not, with obvious results. I have been told that where
instruction is being given, women are crowding to
receive it; but our statesmen have not so much as set
in motion any serious enquiry into the problem. It is
one of those questions which arouse bitter hostility from
the Churches and are of too broad a bearing, too remote
in their consequences, to catch immediate votes. But
it should be the duty of governments to educate, as well
as to court, their constituents, and, above all, not to be
afraid. It is absurd that, when the majority of intelligent
citizens are in favour of family planning, the political
parties should still timorously avoid the subject.

Another question which both parties, to my indignation, refuse to put in the forefront is that of a world
police. You would have thought that after the adventure
at Suez, all responsible statesmen in the free half of the
world would have recognised the necessity for reconsti-

tuting U.N.O. and of giving to it armed force enough to crack down upon the world's naughty "small boys" who have more, not less, freedom for mischief since the H-bomb has permanently frozen the powers of the prefects to use the cane. True, before you have a police you must have a criminal law, but to draft an International Criminal Code should not be beyond our wits: and, having got one, police action would be automatic when "crimes" were committed. By a police I do not mean of course Mr Hammerskjöld's toy soldiers. I mean a mobile force of all arms and great strength. We should have to pool forces and to surrender some measure of sovereignty to achieve it. But, beyond a vague speech or two, nothing has been done. The fact that the Russian government won't play is insufficient excuse; the Western Powers could, if they had the will, enlist a formidable and effective task-force. Much of the trouble is, I suspect, that politicians in power are grossly overworked. They have no time to think. But for Prime Ministers (or American Secretaries of State) to allow themselves to be overworked is in itself a grave fault. They should carefully read Lord Montgomery's *Memoirs*, buy a caravan, have a reliable Chief of Staff to represent them in the Commons, and, instead of spending hours on the front Bench discussing labels and envelopes, pace up and down in front of their caravan and meditate upon the increase of populations, the future of half-baked democracies, and the means of keeping the peace. Nor need a Prime Minister pace alone. Let the pick of the Cabinet be relieved of departmental duties, given ten thousand a year and a caravan apiece, and told to forget the next election and look ahead ten, twenty or even fifty years. And since a politician who has achieved front rank must necessarily have had no leisure for thought for a very long time, our caravanners should not be above taking advice from those who have had such leisure. Non-political persons of ripe minds have been called upon for their thoughts when the country has been at war; there should be no hesitation in making use of them at all times. I admire the laboriousness and the integrity of our public men. I blame them only for not putting first things first.

To jump from politicians to dullness is, perhaps, the result of a natural association of ideas. Whether dull people dislike dullness it is hard to say. Perhaps their own dullness is the result of not knowing what the thing is: for their sakes we must hope so. We are most of us dull to somebody or other. I have a vivid recollection of climbing the stairs with my wife at a party given by Lady Astor, and hearing our hostess, after a quick glance over the banisters, say to her neighbour: "Here come the dullies!" Lady Astor could not be dull if she tried, and we entirely saw her point. But it is not only people who are dull (and for some dull people I have a far deeper affection than for many amusing ones). Most forms of impersonal dullness can, with age and experience, be dodged. No grown-up person need read *Peveril of the Peak* or *The Monastery* which were forced upon me in my tender youth. Nor need I look at the supplements on Trade or Canada which are so generously enclosed, on occasions, in my copy of *The Times*. Or at chairmen's speeches at annual meetings, even when a portrait of the chairman is inset. Club bores can be avoided or, preferably, made the occasion for practising a little kindness. All dull reading-matter, and most dull speeches or sermons, are there to be taken or left.

But there are some kinds of dullness against which I
rebel, all the more perhaps when the blame for them
cannot be precisely imputed. Talk about railway-trains,
for instance, and junctions; it springs up suddenly, even
among intelligent persons, and goes on and on. So does
talk about traffic-jams and parking-places. Health and
doctors are most trying subjects, the more so because it
is difficult not to join in, and to listen to oneself being
dull is devastating. The exchange of recipes between
women is a dreadful thing to overhear. So is conversation about clothes or dressmakers. But the dullness of
things heard lies, I think, less heavily on the spirits than
the dullness of things seen. It is easier to withdraw the
attention from chatter than from dreary spectacles.
When the Liberty horses are mincing with unnatural
gait around the circus ring, with plumes on their heads,
watch them you must; but oh, what bores they are!
How incredibly badly elephants play cricket! They are
not perhaps, minute for minute, duller to watch than
professional cricketers stone-walling, but at least the
men have skill and aptitude. The poor elephant, with
a tiny bat held in his trunk, and a tinier cricket-cap on
his skull, looks and, being an intelligent beast, probably
feels, a fool. But even if he is happy and content, he plays
a wretched game, and it is hard to sit through it.

Films of Morris dancers, and of those parties of young
men and girls from the mountainous regions of Europe,
who dance national dances in national dress, put a great
strain upon me. The dances are often brisk and rhyth-
mical, and, for a few minutes at a time, could be a
pleasure to watch. But these kinds of dancers never tire,
nor do the men who film them ever tire. The whirling
pigtails, the stout round legs, the braid and the brogues:

the camera moves from one to another and back again, insatiable, regardless. The dancers all have wonderful teeth and superb health; you can almost see the international goodwill flashing from their eyes; they are wholesome and eager and not Swiss; but they will not stop. I have thought that they were just about to stop; I have, even for a second, believed that they had stopped; but I have been wrong. It all begins again.

Of all visual dullness, I am not sure that some landscapes are not the most lowering. I am not thinking of the melancholy we feel at seeing the countryside stained and degraded by the works of man; that is more than boredom; it is downright sadness, which can turn to irritation and even to fury. Nor is what is called a "desolate" landscape necessarily dull; a flat and featureless prospect can be redeemed by a compensating expanse of sky, by the spell of far horizons and the sense of space. I have been fascinated by the Canadian prairies; I have not seen, but should like to see, the great deserts of the world. What really gets me down is a landscape of endless small fir-trees or pines, unresponsive to the seasons, impervious to the touch of spring or autumn, too insignificant to be gloomy, dear only to Forestry Commissioners. Is my distaste due only to childhood memories of Camberley Heath, and the convalescent walks I took there, on white and dusty tracks, among those odious undersized conifers, after mumps and measles? I do not think so. The great middle belt of Canada, through which the Canadian Pacific trains lumber for days on end, has nothing in common with Camberley or Aldershot or Bordon. It is a country of a thousand lakes, of rocks and ridges and ravines, a 'big' country. But the shores, the islands, the ridges, the slopes are everywhere clothed with the same lack-lustre, unchanging green of fir-trees. It is dull on a huge, over-powering scale, and the trees are responsible. Bare rocks, with their shadows, their reflections, their shimmering, and their responsiveness to air and light, are never dull. It is their stolid green overcoats that overwhelm the traveller with ennui. I have been fir-ridden in the Austrian mountains; I shall never risk the Black Forest, and I have a feeling that even salmon-fishing in Norway may have to be dearly paid for.

Many will feel about my sufferings from fir-trees what an old Norfolk friend of mine would have felt, had I dared confess it to him, about my attitude to the fat-stock prices on the B.B.C., which to him were the height of pleasurable excitement, for all that he was an old blind pensioner who had never owned a pig. For boredom, of course, is subjective. And I am inclined to think that it is only felt acutely by children. No dullness has ever afflicted me to compare with that I suffered from being driven through the lanes in a slow pony-cart, or seated on the small seat in a victoria, back to the horses, when my mother drove out to leave cards upon a neighbour. Children, full of imagination when left to play games by themselves, have no interior resources when it is a question of sitting still. To this day the smell of hot leather, or the sight of dusty brambles by the roadside, can, for a moment, almost persuade me that life is pointless. And I think the common expression "bored to tears" bears me out. To a child it is no exaggeration.

Aristides must have felt the Athenians to be more than "vinegary" when they ostracised him through weariness at hearing him called "the Just," and we all have a

private Aristides or two of our own. One of mine is
A. E. Housman, in spite of some lines and stanzas as
fine, in their aptness and economy, as anything in English
verse. Another is Shelley's celebrated "Ode to a Skylark." At the very start, "Bird thou never wert" makes
a hideous noise to me, and to find "heart" rhymed with
"wert," fashionable as it would be today, jars me badly.
And then comes:

In profuse strains of unpremeditated art.

To make this line scan, you must pronounce "profuse"
as "proff-use," which is bad enough; but to understand
how art can be unpremeditated is beyond me. It is a
contradiction in terms. In the next stanza Shelley
compares an ascending lark, that tiny, diminishing
speck, to a "cloud of fire." This seems to me to be a
simile worthy of Mr Robert Montgomery. Clouds are
made of vapour, not fire, which is their natural enemy,
and anything less like a cloud, be it made of what it may,
than the compact and exiguous body of a skylark it is
hard to imagine. After this evidence that Shelley had
already lost sight of the skylark altogether—as well he
may have—it is less surprising to find him making it
"run" in the air; but he needed a rhyme for "sun." In
the sixth and seventh stanzas Shelley makes moonlight
loud and, to increase our wonder, melody visible. He
goes on to compare the neat little song-bird to a high-
born maiden, a glowworm, and a rose. And for the
sake of a rhyme to "thine" tells us that he had never
heard praise of "love or wine" that panted forth a flood
of "rapture so divine." Or did he really equate wine with
love? Am I being captious? I do not think so. Shelley's
"Night" is perfect, and he was a great, if not a supreme,

poet, but the Skylark really will not do. A simile can lift verse to the heights, but it must, above all, be apt.

Another private Aristides of my own is cricket. Not the game, which I love to watch and would have dearly loved to play, but "cricket" as standing for fair play and loyal team-work. In fact, from the nature of the case, team-work is less practicable in cricket than in any other game except golf. To be selfish when rowing in an eight or four is impossible, whatever Ouida may have written about her hero rowing faster than the others in the boat. In football selfishness can be exhibited, but not for long: the three-quarter who persists in sticking to the ball when his clear duty is to pass will soon be dropped from the side. But I have sometimes put to myself the following question: "You are the captain of the Eton XI. The night before the Harrow match the Archangel Gabriel, or rather the Devil in his guise, appears at your bedside and gives you the following choice. Either Eton shall beat Harrow, but you yourself will make a brace of ducks, miss three catches, and run out, by your folly, your best batsman; or, Harrow shall win, but you yourself will make a couple of centuries, take six wickets and cover yourself with glory. Which alternative do you choose?" I should like to be sure that I should plump for victory and personal disgrace. But should I? I can think of no other game involving a team in which so cruel a dilemma could be posed, even by Satan himself. There must be many a cricketer who has returned from a lost match in a glow of self-satisfaction, or from a victory in deep depression.

Again, how can a game involve genuine team-work when during its whole course nine members of the batting side are sitting, impotent spectators, in the pavilion? And the remaining pair, out in the middle of the ground, each dependent upon nothing but his own skill and resource? The fielders can "back up," but a catch comes to a single pair of hands—the rest can only stand and pray.

Lastly, the fortunes of a game of cricket can be changed by the weather. Rain can save a side from defeat; a hot sun on a drying wicket can favour the bowlers unfairly. Are these accidents which cause victory or defeat in despite of the true merit of the sides deplored by cricketers? On the contrary, they are devoutly prayed for by those whose side they are likely to help.

For these reasons I find it irritating to hear cricket cited as the best of all "character-makers," and the supreme illustration of "playing for the side." And although "fair play" is unquestionably the rule, I cannot forget that the greatest of cricketers, W. G. Grace, was noted for his wiles and ruses and trickiness. The great man's game, if the stories are true, was by no means always "cricket." It was left to this generation, and to Mr Stephen Potter, to find another name for it: gamesmanship.

Cricket has, none the less, one great advantage over a game like association football: it is played seriously only in the British Commonwealth. It is terrifying to think of a world in which cricket, or for that matter baseball, were to become an international game. I can remember when Larwood almost caused Australia to secede from the Empire: imagine the effect of body-line bowling upon Moscow! It may be objected that soccer is played between nations, and that the opportunities for foul play and trickiness are far greater in that game of tripping and charging. I would reply that in the first place it is by no means certain that these international games of football do not do more harm than good; and, secondly, that, for all its greater popularity, football has none of the symbolic significance, not far removed from that of the Flag or the Monarchy, that cricket has for Englishmen. I think we have fooled ourselves over that excellent game, but the thing has been done; cricket is something that important and intelligent personages can refer to as part of our "heritage" in after-dinner speeches. As far as armaments go, we have already had to resign our claim to be a first-class power. But if ever the day comes when the final of a series of international Test Matches is played out between America and Russia (with the Americans batting on a sticky wicket skilfully prepared by Russian scientists), all Englishmen will feel, for the first time, that they are no longer a first-class people.

As it is, I am opposed to all formal international contests. I do not mean that I would exclude foreign entries from Henley Regatta, or from Wimbledon or from the Open Golf Championship. The relation of guests to hosts and the fact that the visitors represent clubs or themselves, and not their country as a whole, makes a saving difference. But at the Olympic Games the honour of a nation, not the prowess of an individual or a team, is supposed to be at stake, and I cannot accept the position that the prestige of civilised peoples, so various in their gifts and capacities, should be entrusted to a boxer or a hurdler. That the spirit of the Olympic Games has improved during my lifetime I readily admit; I can remember when runners were elbowed off the track and lumps of flesh bitten out of a boxer's chest by his opponent. But I still feel, when each Olympiad comes round, a certain trepidation, and, when all is safely over, a difficulty in sharing either triumph or despondency. Our one gold medal won by a horse at Helsinki amused but did not console me, as it seems to have consoled the press, for defeats which did not, in my opinion, call for consolation. I like to hear of a British victory, of course; but I am far more concerned with getting through the Games without 'incidents' or bad feeling. And neither success nor failure in throwing a discus seems to me relevant to the standing and character of an ancient and versatile race.

And now, having played the superior person long enough, I must make a confession. Should any of you chance to visit the Mound stand at Lord's during the Eton and Harrow match, you will see there an elderly party, beautifully dressed, watching each ball with absorbed attention, and at times swaying (like the Athenians at Syracuse as they watched from the shore the destruction of their ships) this way and that in an agony of hope or fear. In his heart is a black, implacable hostility towards the Harrow players, whose very caps he detests as outlandish; fair play and generosity are not in him; his partisanship is as shameful as it is shameless. And that elderly party will be, ungrammatically, me.

A lifelong grievance of mine has been against myself for not being able to play that admirable game bridge. It is not just that I am unhandy with those small, slippery pieces of pasteboard and find difficulty in picking them up, in arranging them in my hand according to suits, in dealing or shuffling. The basic trouble is that I cannot remember what cards have been played. Once a trick has been turned over and gathered up, it is consigned, as far as I am concerned, to oblivion. It might have been dropped into the waters of Lethe. It is not lack of attention on my part; on the contrary, I strain so hard to remember, that even after a game of family bridge, played for love, I cannot sleep for hours. It was bad enough in the old day of contract bridge when, as far as I remember, there were no "conventions" to be recollected. Of those I have never been able to see the point. Why, if you wish to tell both your partners and your opponents about the state of your hand, must you do so by saying "Two clubs" or "Three diamonds" when that is the very last thing you mean? When everybody understands the "conventions," why not say straight out, in plain English, whatever it is the "convention" signifies? It would at least relieve poor memories like mine of part of the burden.

This lack of card-sense would be humiliating, but for one thing. It has been shared by men of outstanding ability. I have played bridge with Mr Asquith and Lord Milner, and I can honestly say that I was a better player than either of these great men. My game with Mr Asquith cost me two pounds, for he liked to play the hand, and called "Three spades" when he held five small spades to the knave. We were doubled and went down. Two pounds was a small price to pay for the privilege of being partner to a Prime Minister whose kindliness, humour and gusto cast out all fear from the bridge-table. And a lesser price still for the comfort it has been to know that a fine and subtle brain can be unequal to coping with the game of bridge. About Lord Milner's game I have no precise recollection; only that, after several rubbers, I despised it. He was not in my class. A delightful man to play with, charming, easy, and human, but no card-player. I like to think that I was once in a position to look down upon Lord Milner. All the same, I wish I could play bridge.

I have had other complaints against myself which have rankled for shorter or longer periods. One that has been forgotten since I was thirty was that my height and weight, quite apart from my impecuniosity, prevented me from riding in steeplechases. There can be few experiences, for sheer exhilaration, to beat riding fast over fences, and my ambition would have been to enjoy it without declining into horsiness. I did once start on a steeplechase, more hopefully than wisely, for my horse was an undersized charger allotted to me as a machine-gun company-commander in an Infantry Division, a spirited little animal, but not up to my weight. About forty of us lined up, and the first fence, which was a tolerably stiff one, was broad enough to allow at most thirty riders to jump together, knee to knee. Most of us were greenhorns, and we thought, as one man, that since there would be no room to jump together, the thing was to be over first. Did Mr Arthur Benson's motto, which was carried over his schoolroom door at Eton: "Somebody must be last, but nobody need be," ring in our ears? At any rate, we all raced helter-skelter for the fence, and a pretty mess we made of it. My little horse fell on his nose and I on the point of a shoulder. When a week later I was lying in a Belgian schoolroom—a prisoner of war, shot through the chest and back—it was that shoulder, not the serious wounds, that caused me most pain. In the sleepless, aching nights I had time to wonder whether, when a German attack is hourly expected, a steeplechase is really a good idea.

A far more serious grievance, amounting to real resentment, concerns my lack of head for heights. For it has cost me, not the occasional and brief ecstasy of the steeplechaser, but what I believe to be the finest sport in the world: Alpine climbing. I do not know that I have felt profound envy of any other class of men, but of climbers I have been envious indeed. I read and re-read the books of such writers as the late Geoffrey Winthrop Young, of C. F. Meade, of André Roch, not merely with excitement, but with the rueful feeling that those of us who cannot climb mountains have been cheated of a higher satisfaction, both of body and mind, than can be achieved in any other way. I do not mean that I am spartan enough to long for the prolonged disciplines of Mount Everest, or the North Col's icy blizzards. Nothing would induce me to hang suspended from *pitons* on the north wall of the Eiger. It is the climbing of such men as I have mentioned, done for fun, for exhilaration, for the sense of mind and muscle at full stretch, for access to regions of incomparable beauty, of silence and solitude, that I should so dearly have loved to share. I feel it to be an unfair deprivation that I have never been the companion of such guides as the two Lochmatters, of Pierre Blanc, of Josef Knubel. There is a completeness about such men, a perfected fitness, moral and physical, for their vocation, which reminds me, curiously enough, of such professional animals as collies or gun-dogs. The comparison is only in respect of their unconscious and instinctive reactions to the physical problems of high mountaineering, and perhaps to a kind of dog-like fidelity, for these guides, as human beings, are fine fellows indeed. We who have never known them have missed, I feel sure, something rare and encouraging. It has not been enough, for me, to read about them. I should like to have moved in their company, supple and confident, up the great precipices of the Grépon to look down, unflinchingly, upon the Mer de Glace.

As it is, I tremble all over when I stand upon a chair to fix an electric bulb, and I have never reached, because of the way my knees knock together, the top of my own library-ladder. It is not merely humiliating; it has cut me off from what I believe to be the acme of human enjoyment.

If I conclude, with this last grudge, my catalogue of enmities and dislikes, some reader may be shocked by my omissions. Can you really, he will say, be so poor-spirited, so feebly tolerant, as not to share my dislike of the X.Y., of Mr A., of that dreadful B.? But I do, I do. It is true that I read the X.Y., but mainly, as a friend said of another newspaper, to make my blood boil once a week. It improves the circulation. And as for Mr A. and that dreadful B., Celt as I am, I have a strain of caution in me, and libel actions, even if won on a plea of justification, are expensive things. Besides, I have, I hope, said enough to achieve my object, which was to prove to Mr Raymond Mortimer that an admixture of vinegar is, after all, to be found in my veins.

## CHAPTER XX

# GOING ABROAD

I FIRST went abroad too early and for too long.
Children neither lift up their eyes to the hills nor
enjoy walking up them; their palates are unadventurous, their sense of smell acute and fastidious; they
are conventional, shy, and herd-loving. I have never
again been so British, so insular, so marmalade-minded,
as I was from my eleventh to my thirteenth year, when
being carted about by parental poverty and *Wanderlust*
from Switzerland to Provence and back again. I wanted
ponds and lawns and plumbing, and to walk on the flat
without looking where I trod.

A permanent home at Valescure changed all that.
At thirteen a boy's eyes, I suppose, begin to open; the
*maquis* all about my father's villa was fragrant and
clean, and in a warm sea, to which we coasted downhill
on our bicycles, we found exhilaration in exile. Even so,
I still envied my schoolfellows who did not start their
holidays from Newhaven. I was a bad sailor; but when
my father discovered that the longer sea-passage from
Newhaven to Dieppe was an economy, I could say
nothing, for economy was a law of our being. The
return-journey from Dieppe was by night, and there
was a saloon with plush sofas for the second-class
passengers, but the smell of it brought on nausea even
when the sea was calm, and I crouched all night by the

funnel, where warm air came up through a grating.
From Paris to St Raphael it was also a night-journey
both ways, sitting up, and the longer my back grew the
more violent the migraines that ensued. The letters
P.L.M. woven into a grubby antimacassar were to
me, for nearly a decade, a hateful symbol.

It was on one of these night-journeys, when I was all
but a young man, that I learnt the kind of thing the
French believe about us. I was in a corner seat, with
seven Frenchmen as companions. Before trying to sleep,
I opened the window; there was an immediate clamour.
The night air, they affirmed, was lethal. I argued that
since we all slept with our windows open in England,
yet survived, this could hardly be true. I was overborne,
and the window was closed. When the blue shade was
pulled down over the lamp and I closed my eyes, my
fellow-travellers, like T. E. Browne's hawthorn, began
to whisper about me.

"*Il a rigolé, ce jeune homme?*"

But no, said one who had been to England, he was not
joking. The English do sleep with their windows open,
"*mais, comme les Marseillais, ils dorment la tête dessous le
matelas. Donc, rien ne les touche!*"

I wonder how many people know that the people of
Marseilles sleep with their heads under the mattress?
But I firmly believed that I was being poisoned, and not
until twenty years later did I learn the truth about open
windows from Robin Rayleigh, the distinguished
scientific son of a celebrated father. "The amount of
poisonous gas breathed out by eight people in a closed
railway carriage for twelve hours would be about one
teaspoonful, and the effects negligible." It is not "bad"
air, it is the lack of movement of air upon our skins that

makes us feel uneasy in a closed railway-carriage. With a fan working we should be comfortable enough. Since learning this, I have enjoyed the snugness of sleeping with closed windows on winter nights.

It was on the P.L.M., on a later occasion, that I was rebuked by a ticket-collector, and noticed, for the first time, the contrast between the vocabularies used by Frenchmen and Englishmen in comparable walks of life. In a crowded train I had left a suitcase in the corridor, there being no room for it on the rack.

"*Je n'aime pas cet égoisme là*," said the ticket-collector. "*Quand vous, Monsieur, un homme énorme, voyagez, faut avoir des égards aux autres.*"

I feel sure that no British Railway servant would have mentioned egoism, or pointed out the special obligations of bulky travellers.

It was from the Gare de Lyon that I drove away in a fiacre one foggy morning, so dazed with headache that I left my portmanteau on the platform. Only when I reached the Gare du Nord did I discover my neglect. There was nothing for it but to rattle back over the cobbles, through those endless shabby streets, to retrieve the thing. My journey-money, calculated to the last sixpence, allowed for one, not two, crossings of Paris; I could not ask for more, and a serious inroad was made upon my pocket-money for the next half. But I caught the train for Dieppe by a few minutes, the cabman, kinder to me than to his horse, having entered into my anxieties and made a galloping affair of the second journey.

Four times a year, for nearly a decade, I travelled between home and school or college over the same route, but seeing nothing of France between Paris and

Avignon, a countryside, for me, of eternal night. The rolling hedgeless fields of the Pas de Calais I knew, and the reed-beds and mistletoe-ridden poplars around Abbeville; I was familiar with the stony wastes of the Crau and the limestone hills of Toulon. I dreaded and disliked the journey, with its seasickness and the cramped and fitful snatches of uneasy sleep beneath that blue-shaded lamp. So that it speaks much for the native enchantment of France herself and of her inhabitants, so alien yet so fascinating, that, in spite of such memories, I never land at Calais or Boulogne without a thrill. The very sight of the blue blouses of the porters, and the sound of their Latin voices as they infiltrate the herd of passengers, induce a pleasing expectancy. And the first taste of French food in the dining-car is none the worse for the menu being unvarying and predictable. The glass of red wine, that must be lifted for filling because of the shaking of the train, is more than ordinarily potent to warm and to release, through its promise of wines to come. Food and drink, for several weeks, are going to be a main, if not the principal, source of pleasure. It is a reflection that goes well with a cigar.

Nowadays this flutter of excitement on landing in France is merely a prelude to Italian holidays, but I would not miss it for anything. To hear a little French spoken, to speak a few words of French, if only to a porter and a dining-car attendant, is to renew an ancient acquaintance and to get on terms, in the very anteroom, with the Continental way of life. France, for this reason, would always be my chosen gateway to the rest of Europe. Landing at the Hook of Holland is a flat business in comparison, with no welcome to the ear. One enters Germany by that route like a deaf man entering a strange house. I first went to Berlin in 1912, on business for Holophane Ltd, the makers of prismatic glassware. It was the Kaiser's Berlin, and the beer was delicious, but if you wished to drink it with your luncheon in the Tiergarten, you must descend to a lower terrace and be content with a cheaper lunch before it could be served. That, at least, was the rule; but the head waiter, having made a great fuss, turned out to be corruptible and finally gave us a light beer in champagne-glasses, to preserve appearances. In our ignorance we felt the Germans to be an absurd, not a dangerous, people, an impression increased by my experience in a tram-car. It was a low car, open at the sides, with a centre gangway and all the seats facing forwards. The roof was supported by iron stanchions rising from the backs of the seats. I was seated in an outside corner-seat when the conductor, passing down the centre, paused, pointed at my feet, and rapped out what sounded like a peremptory command. I glanced at my feet, could see nothing abnormal about them except their size, which was irremediable, and shook my head to express my lack of understanding. The conductor stopped the car. Fleshy necks were craned in my direction. He again pointed at my shoes and this time gave me a longer lecture, not one word of which could I understand. People were now gathering on the pavement. The conductor next ordered me out of the tram. "*Aus*" was a word I knew; in any case his gesture of dismissal was unmistakable. I had paid my fare and I sat still. The little crowd on the pavement grew bigger. The passengers began to jabber at me. I went on sitting still. The driver alighted and came to see what was afoot. He found it was two feet, and at once took the conductor's part. I still sat still. Two policemen, noticing the crowd on the pavement, intervened. The conductor appealed to them, and they, too, ordered me out. I I shook my head. The policemen entered the car and attempted to pull me out by main force. I put one arm round the iron stanchion at my side, gripped it tight, and became immoveable. The policemen were little men; I was a big one; the struggle was unequal. They admitted defeat and left the car. Deserted by his allies, the conductor could do no more. The driver went back to his seat and we proceeded. Later, a German who spoke good English mounted the car. The story was told to him by the outraged passengers. He then explained to me that my legs were crossed, which was "*verboten.*" I uncrossed them, and the incident was closed.

This was the first time I won a victory over Germany; the second occasion was a year later, in the giant ship *Vaterland*, when I knocked Captain von Perth, of the Imperial Guard, off a pole with a cushion. I represented the British Empire, a responsibility I felt so keenly that I believe I got my blow in a fraction of a second before the word "go," remembering the old adage:

> Well for the fighting man whose cause is just,
> But he fights best who gets his blow in fust.

If so, the umpire failed to spot it, and I toppled von Perth with a single bang, to my immense relief. This was in June 1914, and my adversary, who was a charming fellow, assured us that war between our two countries was out of the question. But my father-in-law, Lord Grey, with whom we were travelling home from New York, had characteristically struck up an acquaintance with a big bearded German Socialist on the second-class deck. "Do not listen," this man had said to him, "to what those Junkers up there are telling you. Our Kaiser and his Generals have decided that you are a decadent nation, and mean war. You will see." In a couple of months we did see.

Our party was in the *Vaterland* because it was the maiden voyage of that great ship, then the biggest in the world. We had booked cabins in the *Empress of Ireland*, sailing from Quebec, but a telegram from the owners of the *Vaterland* to my father-in-law, offering him the royal suite for the return-journey from New York, at the ordinary fare, was too tempting to refuse. It was a lucky change of plan for us all, for when we were two days out from New York news was received by wireless that the *Empress of Ireland* had been sunk through collision in the St Lawrence, with heavy loss of life. A director of the German line that owned the *Vaterland* was on board, and I shall never forget the expression on his sabre-cut face when he came to tell us the news. "And vat is very terrible," he added, "is zat it is belieft zat de officers and crew saved demselves, and left de passengers to draun!" The gleam in his Teutonic eyes was devilish. "Jost fancy, in a Briddish ship!" We were indignant and told him that such things did not happen. "Let us ho-ope so," he said. It was, of course, pure moonshine. But what other nation could have produced a creature capable of announcing a tragedy to his guests in such language?

Twenty-three years were to go by before I was again in Germany (for I do not count lying in a prison hospital in Pomerania as being "abroad"). By this time I knew them to be a dangerous people, and, as luck would have it, when motoring through Munich on our return from Austria in 1937, we were held up by endless columns of marching troops. Although it was summer, they were in greatcoats and steel helmets and carried enormous knapsacks; they were young, and looked exhausted and sullen. But their march-discipline was perfect, and there was something sinister about their sweaty, depressed young faces. "Cannon-fodder" was the word that came to mind; had they looked more cheerful, one might have been less conscious of the ruthlessness of the man who made them march. This was in 1937, and I wished that our appeasing politicians at home could have shared my glimpse of them. Between Munich and the Swiss frontier, the landscape itself was minatory: armies of black fir-trees, in columns and squares, all dressed in lines, rigid and at attention, dotted the rolling plain. The very woods and forests appeared to be on manœuvres.

Of the Salzkämmergut in Austria we had seen little through the incessant, shrouding rain, and the gloomy monotony of the pine-forests, darkening every mountainside, got me down. We had a glimpse of Prince Starhemberg, a proud, athletic figure, off to climb the great rock-wall that rises sheer from the Altaussee at its eastern end, to remind us that the friendly café-dancers in *lederhosen* might be, as before in history, dancing on a volcano. And there was one glorious day of sunshine and colour when we visited the Wolfgangsee, and rowed across the sky-blue lake to behold, lunching among humans at the White Horse Inn, Apollo himself. He wore a dark-blue sweater and polo-breeches: hair, eyes, features, figure, bearing, all were godlike and not quite credible. If we stared more than was polite, he must have been accustomed to it. As a profound admirer of Mr P. G. Wodehouse, I was enchanted to discover that this lordly and beautiful being was called Wooster.

This was my first and last visit to Europe in a car, and we came home through Switzerland and France. It was a curious experience to turn aside in Argau to visit Schloss Wildegg, the feudal fortress in which I had spent my twelfth summer. The suits of armour still stood in the Rittersaal, but the scale of everything was sadly diminished. Mediaeval castles sited and built for defence should be admired from below, not visited. I could recall, on the spiral staircases and in the narrow chambers of a dull provincial museum, nothing of the romance, still less the shudders, that a boy had found in them long ago.

Far more exciting was our discovery of Morat, on the main road from Zürich to Lausanne, east of Lake Neuchâtel. "Why were we never told about Morat?" was our question as we drove through a fortified gate in fifteenth-century walls to find ourselves in what must be one of the most perfect small, walled towns in Europe. The main source of delight lies in the arcaded streets, and the perfect proportions of the houses. The arcades cannot, as in Italy and the south, have been built against the sun; the main street is of a generous width and the houses of two, or at most three, storeys. Everything is on a small scale. You derive a pleasure in Morat from the moderate dimensions of the buildings, akin to that afforded by the Horse Guards; and experience the same sense of inevitability as is given by classical music. I have been there but once, and that over twenty years ago, but no reader, if I have any, shall complain that he was never told about Morat. Another discovery on our homeward journey was Dijon, hitherto nothing but a disturbing cry in the middle of the night during those racking journeys on the P.L.M. A great clanking railway-station, that was Dijon for me. So it was an excitement to find street after street of eighteenth-century "hotels," with pitched roofs, dormer windows and exquisite wrought-iron balconies, showing up, by their dignity and simplicity, the fantastically bedizened dwelling of Diane de Poitiers. As for the crayfish cooked in burgundy, and the burgundy itself that we drank in balloon-like goblets of thinnest glass, I remember them through the warm, muzzy haze in which we walked off our lunch among those highbred thoroughfares.

If Dijon made us mellow, the cathedral at Laon enraptured us. It stands on a bluff nearly six hundred feet above the plain and, externally, is all of a piece. Built in the twelfth century, with rounded arches throughout, it has a lightness and grace seldom seen in our own more thickset Norman fanes. The windows are of plain glass, so that the interior, which is entirely free, with one major exception, from the accretions of mediaeval or modern piety which so often bedevil great churches, is all lightness and space. The architecture is seen naked, scoured and unashamed. The one later addition miraculously comes off. For the side-chapels are enclosed with Renaissance screens in white marble, intricately sculptured and arabesqued. The contrast between the high austerity of the whole and the light-hearted decoration of the chapels is, by some trick of proportion, not only acceptable but enjoyable. I am ashamed to say that I had forgotten, until lately reminded, one charming touch. The gargoyles are the graven heads of oxen in

memory of the patient beasts who hauled the stones for
the builder up that formidable bluff from the plain.
From Laon to the sea we traversed some of the battle-
fields of the first World War, but, without careful
search, there was little by which to recognise them.
Villages that had been entirely destroyed were now as
completely restored, but in a lamentable style. There
had been a few buildings of red and white brick,
hideously patterned, in most of these villages before the
war, the school, for instance, or an estaminet. But the
daub-and-plaster of the houses and cottages, tiled or
thatched, had, however ramshackle, been not un-
pleasing. Now, the raw red and white bricks lined the
village streets with monotonous repetition, merciless to
the eye. I was reminded of that character in one of Harry
Graham's books, who had a great deal of taste, all of it
bad.

Finding ourselves near Bapaume, which I had last
seen in ruins, I had the idea of showing my wife the
spot on which I had been shot, and lain for thirty-six
hours, during the retreat of the Third Army in March
1918. Thanks to a railway-cutting, over the rim of
which the head and shoulders of the German who
bagged me had suddenly popped up, at about twenty-
five yards' range, the place was easy to identify. But
there was no obelisk, not even a stone, to mark it. My
wife herself did not suggest planting a peg there. Only
those who have themselves been shot could think this
resort to a ploughed field in France other than rather
absurd.

When summing up my experiences of France, they
amount to so little that I have difficulty in accounting
for my profound feeling of intimacy with a country

with which, in fact, I am barely acquainted. I suppose a Provençal home in boyhood, and many months' meandering with the Cavalry from village to village in rear of the battle-lines, has given me a sense of familiarity out of proportion to the actual scope of my explorations. But there it is; France and the French, whatever their political antics, can never for me be "foreign" as the other countries and peoples of Europe are foreign. It is not just that I have spoken their language, can read their books, and appreciate their art of living: the familiarity I feel is with the very soil and landscape, with the poplars, the roofs, the shutters, even with PERNOD on the blank end-wall of too tall, too narrow a house. I revel in the smell of roasting coffee, in the incessant tinkling of a bell at wayside stations; in the gesticulations, the forefinger drawn across the nose with every *"Figurez-vous!"*; in the sonorous male voices; in the fine phrases that even a peasant uses as a matter of course. I delight in the thumbnail sketches of *Actualités* on the front page of the wretchedly printed newspapers:

'A DEAUVILLE'

*"Je viens de rencontrer ma femme"*
*"Tiens! Comme le monde est petit."*

I enjoy the sight of the placid fishermen who line the river-banks on Sundays, and call their little dog *"Poisson"*—*"parce qu'il ne mord pas,"* and of the breadth and grandeur of the rivers themselves. I am amused, when not its victim, by the French passion for the sublime, whatever their practice. The Englishman who had been grossly overcharged by a cabman in the Midi and had refused to pay was naturally indignant when the

*Juge de paix* addressed him as follows: "*Vous, Monsieur êtes anglais, riche. Lui est français, pauvre. Vous le payerez ce qu'il demande.*" The Englishman protested that there was no justice "*dans ce maudit pays*" but was sternly called to order. The magistrate pointed a solemn forefinger to the skies: "*La justice, Monsieur, est éternelle, immuable.*" That could never have been said from the bench in Surrey, but might not a Surrey county court be a livelier place if such things could be said? Fine sentiments, no doubt, come too easily to the French. But are we, as a people, enriched by the fact that, except to Sir Winston Churchill, they never come to us at all?

Be that as it may, the French are articulate and enjoy their own language, and it is a pleasure to listen to them, even when, as on the stage, they talk too fast for us to follow. "You must move your mouth," my mother used to tell us, as children, when teaching us French, and she was right. They do move their mouths, and pronounce all their consonants, a thing which our younger actors and actresses are failing to do. And the men speak in a lower, more manly-sounding key than ourselves. This I learnt, rather to my surprise, during the First World War, when I was able, upon occasions, to contrast the voices of soldiers from Bedfordshire, talking together in dugouts or billets, with those of French peasants. There were no deep chest-notes; no humming of vocal chords, among the light, head-voices of our own people. But the Frenchmen's conversations were resonant and sonorous; they could even "boom" most agreeably to the ear.

With so much that charms and delights in France, I sometimes wonder why we do not linger there and "new loveliness survey," instead of taking, year after year, a sleeping-carriage in the Gare de Lyon and jolting through the night to the great tunnels, the Simplon or the Mont Cenis, that lead to Italy. The reason is partly, no doubt, that to the elderly Briton sunshine and warmth are the main *desiderata*, and that, to make sure of them, you must go south of the Alps, preferably in September. But the irresistible pull of Italy comes not only from the blue sky but from the classic landscape over which that sky so dependably presides. Ilex, olive, cypress, vine—their very names are magical—and between them go the white oxen; backing them are the many-coloured mountains, and in every town or village, white upon the plain or honey-coloured on the hills, you encounter, whether your taste is for buildings or pictures or merely to watch from a shady arcade the motions of a spirited and extra-vert people, almost inexhaustible delights.

Our Italian journeys begin early in February in a London flat, where the Speyer-Jones quartet, companions of a dozen years, meet together, with maps and guide-books, to dine and plan for the following September. Since those who do a thing well mostly enjoy doing it, we take it for granted that Dorothea Speyer will visit the travel-agents, consult the time-tables, write to the innkeepers, estimate the cost, and do all the tiresome business of preparation with relish. It is more than possible that we are wrong, and that she does not enjoy it at all, but undertakes it from pure unselfishness and goodness of heart. On reflection, I cannot remember hearing her say that it was a pleasure to her. We are certainly careful enough not to enquire, feeling that in this case, as in so many, it is more blessed to receive than to give.

The next excitement is at Victoria Station, waiting
for the first sight, in the crowd that streams through the
barrier, of Ferdy Speyer's beret. This beret is a symbol.
It betokens that Ferdy has put off the Imperial Chemical
and Industrial side of his nature and is now a sauntering,
questing, art-loving cosmopolitan. Sometimes the beret
is late in appearing, and we are fretted with anxiety;
sometimes it is early, stationary above an outspread
*Times* at the boat-train's side, and we quicken our steps,
reassured. Victoria Station is an ugly place, unworthy
of a capital city, but when the beret is hoisted and our
destination Dover, it is all charm and romance.

A friend who lived for some years in one of those
houses which crouch beneath the white cliffs of Dover,
has told me that the screaming of the gulls, night and
day, is almost past bearing; but out in the harbour,
while the boat is waiting to sail, the cries of the sea-
birds have an exhilarating holiday sound. But not to
Dorothea, who never hears them, for although the
Channel is always calm in September, she refuses to
tempt Providence and lies prone in a darkened cabin
until, by the silence of the propellers, she knows that
we have arrived. The beret, on the contrary, firmly
planted against the breeze, is to be found on the upper
deck and in the bows, protecting its wearer from the
casual accostings of his fellow-countrymen. For none
of them suppose that its wearer would be likely to
understand English.

Of my private thrill in landing in France I have
already told, and it is in the dining-car between Calais
and Paris that the quartet, necessarily scattered on boat
and in custom-house, is first properly united. So high
are our spirits that we forget at every reunion what we

should know only too well, that you cannot talk in a French dining-car against the roar and rattle of the train. We begin by thinking that our poor friends have become sadly deaf since last year; then we start shouting; in the end we subside into silence, intimating to each other by grimaces and gestures our pleasures in the French dishes. But the silence is an easy one, for we are old friends and have no need to make conversation. The first quality to be sought in a travelling-companion is the negative one of making no social demands; the positive ones that come next are a community of taste and not too great a disparity in physical vigour. Our quartet shares a keen delight in landscape, architecture, paintings and food and, except for Ferdy in a picture-gallery, a consensus of opinion as to when to sit down. Once seated, we take our separate lines as to whether an *espresso*, a *cappuccino* or a *strega* is the best restorative between churches, but we are all agreed that the secret of sightseeing is to rest and refresh between sights. The visual arts make extraordinary demands upon the body, which not even the keenest delight and excitement can override, and the sigh of relief with which one sinks into a café chair after a tour of S. Zanipolo is a sign not of indifference to, but of relish for, the things seen. The greater the appreciation, the greater the exhaustion, and the first requisites for sustained aesthetic enjoyment are food and drink.

Sleeping-cars ought to be provided with an extra compartment where husbands can sit while their wives are dressing and undressing, for even the sense of rushing through the night towards an Italian daybreak can hardly make the narrow corridor endurable, and on return-journeys, when the carrot has been eaten, it is a

dreadful place indeed. True, there are little polished
wooden seats that can be let down, and which can just
support one half of the human behind, but they block
the passage when sat upon, and must be lifted for every
passer-by. They tantalise without serving any useful
purpose. But when the Italian daybreak arrives, yellow-
ing the blinds, all discontents are forgotten.

Of the two tunnels that serve the trains from Paris,
the Simplon provides the more dramatic way of
bursting into warmth and sunshine. There is a short
downward rush from the southern mouth of the tunnel,
with glimpses of green alps and Swiss chalets, to
Domodossola, where the train stops, and you lean
from the window to test the climate. The mountains
are still pine-clad, but thereafter the little dark brown
villages have the true Italian bell-towers, and in no time
small vineyards appear, a cypress or two in the ceme-
teries and Spanish chestnuts on the lower slopes. The
valley broadens, the flanking mountains diminish to
foot-hills and at Baveno, Italy is herself. She is the Italy
of the picture-postcards, with true blue hydrangeas
massed in the villa-gardens and the Borromean islands
floating on and reflected in Lake Maggiore. A little self-
conscious and poster-like, no doubt, and far removed
from the ancient, earthy Italy of Umbria or Tuscany,
but, for all that, dramatic and exciting and full of
promise. The Lakes were my first love and I remain
true to them: for those who love a lake and an island
but dislike great hotels and villadom I recommend a
visit to the Albergo at Orta. The island of San Giulio,
to which, in the fourth century, St Julius sailed in a stone
boat to destroy the snakes, is no less beautiful, in all
lights, than the Isola Bella, and, like the Isola Bella, has

the air of a miniature floating city, monkish or patrician, with no visible means of subsistence. Like all islands, it compels one to take a boat and row all round it, as well as to land on it; and from its terraces you look back complacently at Orta and the broad orange-coloured awning beneath which you have been breakfasting and dining, to the envy, no doubt, of the constricted islanders. But this is a book of memories, not a guide-book, and I can never think of Orta without seeing again, in my mind's eye, the three black poodles. They first appeared high above our heads as we started out for a walk; three black curly heads, three red tongues, hanging through an iron railing. From their terrace, twenty feet above the road, they spied us below them, shirt-sleeved, striding, obviously bound for the country, and they barked out an excited suggestion that they should come too. You cannot explain things to a dog on the top of a high wall, and we could only say "hello" and hurry on. The barking ceased, but fifty yards further on there were the three black poodles, this time at ground-level, standing on their hind legs, paws on a cross-bar, begging to be taken. They had raced silently through the dark thickets of a sun-proof garden, behind a shuttered and rather sinister villa backed by a cliff, to renew their appeal face to face. This time we could look into their shining and demanding eyes, but even Ferdy's workaday Italian was unequal to the task of making them understand that we had no key to the heavy, florid iron gate that held them prisoner. But they never lost heart; on our return they were waiting by the gate, and raced up their invisible route to wriggle at us from the terrace and to bark us "Dog speed!" Theirs was the unconquerable hope.

Italy is hardly the country for dog-lovers, and except for a memorable encounter on a hill in the Abbruzzi, when a majestic white Maramman sheepdog stalked across the turf to taste our lunch, I can recall, beside the dear poodles of Orta, only the two bulldogs in Rome. This incomparable pair had the loosest brindled coats, the most endearing snuffles, the most crumpled faces, the flattest and coldest muzzles that could be wished for; but they dwelt in the British Embassy and so can hardly count. Cats are plentiful, and since Ferdy Speyer never passes a cat without talking to it in its own language, our sightseeing is subject to constant interruptions. Eleven cats in one Venetian *cortile*, gracefully disposed among the statuary there displayed for sale, entail a deal of rather trivial chit-chat, in a tongue unknown to the rest of us, but we respect Ferdy's sense of what is due to cats, and are patient. Indeed we go out of our way to point cats out to him, for it is human nature to lose less time over things shown to us than over our own discoveries. Cats that we others have seen first are never actually cut by Ferdy but are more briefly, if no less amicably, greeted.

The Lakes are not for culture-hounds, but for those who enjoy lazing and gazing. They ask nothing of the traveller but to look, and to look; he can forget his guide-book and his Berenson and the Medicis, and spend his days as he would in Cashmere or on the West Coast of Scotland. Whether breakfasting beneath a green pergola at Locarno, or picnicking under Spanish chestnut trees above Varenna, or dining by lamplight among the oleanders of Bellagio, or opening his morning shutters upon the great limestone mountain that faces Torbole, he has no mental exertion to make, no names or dates to remember, nothing to do but to stare, receptive and relaxed, at such landscapes as only mountains, sky and water in conjunction can exhibit. The outlines are often majestic, and the colours, ever shifting, invariably delectable.

Not that strenuous exercise is ruled out; as mere sexagenarians, Ferdy and I have toiled for four and a half hours up Monte Grona behind Menaggio, where I sat upon the turfed and rounded summit to watch Ferdy pick his footsteps, like a mountain goat, up the knife-edge to the crags, and stand there on a pinnacle above precipices which even that old alpine campaigner admitted to be "spectacular." The worst of having, like myself, no head for heights is that one suffers even from watching another person stand poised above the abyss, and I had almost decided the gentlest way of breaking the news to Dorothea and of getting the body off the hill, when Ferdy strolled back to eat his hard-boiled egg. How enviable are those who know that, provided there is a foothold, a handhold, the lack of anything but empty air above, about and beneath them is irrelevant; and who have never known the trembling of the knees, the nausea within and the overpowering impulse to leap into the void which attacks those who, like Dorothea Speyer and myself, keep to the mountainside of a broad carriage-road, however substantial the wall that guards the valley-side.

To become saturated with Italy's landscape before attacking her architecture and pictures is no bad thing; for both were contrived beneath an Italian, not a northern sky, and an arcaded street or a Giorgione pastoral alike proclaim it. In some years we have done our preliminary training not among the Lakes but upon

the west coast. There is a great deal to be said for floating
upon a warm and buoyant Mediterranean sea while you
gaze at the Carrara Mountains, surely one of the most
spell-binding minor ranges in Europe. Streaked with the
débris, which looks like snow, of a thousand years of
marble-quarrying, peaked and accidented and tapering
to tenuous crests of multi-coloured rock, a magnet for
dramatic thunderclouds, the Carraras run parallel to the
sea-coast from near Spezia to Pisa. But they do not rise
from the sea itself; a flat plain, from six to fifteen miles
across, separates their western slopes from the broad
white beaches, and to the eye of a swimmer in the sea,
or to a beach-lizard reclining in a deck-chair beneath a
striped umbrella, they could not be better placed. To
such an eye they rise above the green and level tops of
umbrella-pines, or the flickering greys and whites of
poplars, near enough for the complicated structure of
their bones to be seen, far enough for their mass and
proportion to be appraised.

These strange hills appear even more fantastic in out-
line when seen end-on, from the north; but to enjoy
that aspect you must have the good fortune to know
Mrs Aubrey Waterfield or her son Gordon. For it is
from the ramparts of their castle at Aulla, built in 1500
by a robber-banker from Milan to take toll of rich
travellers, that the marble mountains are seen in their
most theatrical pose. The castle itself stands menacingly
on a rock three hundred feet above the confluence of
two rivers, and its great cool, vaulted rooms carry upon
their heads, by a seeming miracle, the weight not only
of flower-gardens but of an avenue of pines and ilex.
Roof-gardens are one thing, roof-trees, thirty feet high,
are quite another; and, sitting in their shade on a hot and

humming September morning, I believe with difficulty
that I am, in fact, upon a house-top.

Of Lina Waterfield herself I shall not say much, since
friendship between the living imposes its reticences, but
those who have been her guests, whether at Poggio
Gerhardo or at Aulla, will agree with me that if bidden
to choose the most appropriate background for Lina,
we should pick upon one or the other of those two
delectable homes of hers. Equally if bidden to find the
perfect chatelaine for the Castello or the Villa, we should
choose Lina. Endowed with beauty of the sort that,
being in the bone, endures a lifetime, long happily
married to an artist with good looks to rival her own,
heir to the first lady in Florence, the redoubtable Janet
Ross, Bernard Berenson's friend, for years the *Observer's*
Italian correspondent, one of Mussolini's *bêtes-noires*,
Lina unites in herself looks, graces, taste and experience
of uncommon quality. What is more, she has retained
intact that sure sign of a youthful heart, the capacity to
make, and to care about, new friends. Poggio Gerhardo,
half-villa, half-fortress, stands high above the valley of
the Arno on the slopes near Settignano, in a rolling
grey sea of olives. From its terrace, haunted by swallow-
tail butterflies that canvas the blazing zinnias and shaded
by a mighty persimmon tree, you looked westward
down the valley to the Duomo, faint and ethereal in the
morning sunshine or darkly opaque against the sunset
sky. With Lina's own guide to Florence in their pockets,
her guests daily braved the tram which, crowded like
the Bakerloo at rush-hour, carried them twice a day to
that city of treasures, now, alas, made hideous with the
roar and racket of Vespas. What we saw there is too
well known to be mentioned again, with the possible

exception of the Library in the Riccardi Palace. For this exquisite example of Baroque decoration has to be reached by a separate entrance from the street; there is a lift to be taken, and a bell-push to be pushed at the side of a locked door. It needs courage to ring that bell in that secluded lobby; but when rung, it is answered by a surprised Civil Servant in a short black coat and pin-stripe trousers. You begin to apologise, but he politely beckons you to enter, directs you to another door, and leaves you to yourself. There are early printed books and illuminated missals in glass cases, but the glories of the place, the things that exact a gasp of delight, are the bookcases and the gallery which serves them. If there is a high-water mark for sheer elegance, it must surely be here.

I did not shine at the dinner-table on my first evening at Poggio Gerhardo. I was sitting next to a small, dark lady who had been introduced to me as Mrs Davies, and had failed to mark the penetrating and quizzical gleam in her eyes, when John Morris leant across the table, lifted his glass of good red Poggio wine, and said to my neighbour: "I think we should drink to the book's success." We filled our glasses and drank: my neighbour thanked us, and I asked her: "What is the book about?"

"Jane Austen."

"Is it your first?"

"No. I've written several books."

"Biographies?"

"No. Novels."

I read few contemporary novels, and her name meant nothing to me, but it was only good manners to say that I must repair the gap in my reading and to ask for a title.

"I've written quite a few. Perhaps *The Constant Nymph* ?"

She was Margaret Kennedy.

Poggio Gerhardo is now, I believe, a nunnery, and Lina, who was decidedly not cut out to be a nun, would no longer feel at home there. And to us who have known her only in later years the Castello at Aulla will always be her best-remembered background. It was from Aulla that she drove us, past that crenellated castle at Sarzana, like an illustration for a fairy-story, to be introduced to the self-exiled, but not forgotten, doyen of English letters, Percy Lubbock. I ought not, I know, when recalling the privilege of meeting the author of *The Craft of Fiction*, of *Roman Pictures*, of *Earlham*, of *Shades of Eton*, to remember anything trivial, but the day was hot, and the tall glass jug of iced tea with peaches in it was so novel and so refreshing that I cannot entirely disentangle my first memory of our kind host and his pithy talk from the nectar he offered us. Nor, for the matter of that, from his cool and spacious home, with wide loggias and painted Italian furniture, where the twentieth century touches hands with the Renaissance. Gli Scafari is not an ancient house, having been built by its present owner, but it sits on the red rocks among the pines with such an air of authority and permanence, so strong and simple without, so subservient to space within, that it commands all the respect we pay to age. In which regard it differs from its owner who, for all his seniority, and the heavy handicap of partial blindness, retains the lively, questing mind of youth. Sitting, a looming and impressive figure, under his broad loggia, he belies his senatorial appearance with the friendly ease and light touches of his conversation.

## CHAPTER XXI

# THE ORACLES OF GOD

GLI SCAFARI is only a mile or two south of Lerici, where Shelley's villa still stands on the half-moon bay, each horn of which is crowned with an ancient castle. From the front-door of the Hotel Shelley et des Palmes you have but to cross the road, dodging the Vespas, to swim in a warm sea before dinner. Ilex-trees push up from the floor through the ceiling of the restaurant to shade the flat roof, where in the dark pool of their shadows, after bending and dodging through the lines of the hotel's washing, you can sit through the blazing September mornings. It was here, I remember, that I did much of my re-reading of the Old Testament. For elderly travellers books are a necessity, since sightseeing is a killing pursuit, if not judiciously rationed; and when weight and bulk have to be considered, long books are better than short books. The Old Testament is a very long book indeed, and can certainly not have been read by me in a week; yet, for some reason, it is with the long leisurely mornings on that restaurant's roof that I mostly associate my pursuit of Goodness. For that was what I was after: to discover how much such Goodness, in the highest sense, could be found in those Oracles of God which, after nearly seven years of Sunday Questions at Eton, had left so dubious a taste in my mind's mouth. For my purpose

I was not going to count as Goodness any of those virtues without which no society can hold together, even a godless one; I scrutinised every example of "righteousness" to see whether it was of the sort that "paid" in social life, or was of the disinterested and unselfish kind, such as pity, self-sacrifice and loving-kindness.

In the actions attributed to Jehovah (so disastrously translated as "the Lord") I could find little to approve. He is arbitrary, unjust, jealous, vindictive, a wholesale killer, occasionally disgusting, often pitifully pernickety and small-minded. Nor is much Goodness to be found in his favourites and protégés, when they were men of action. Jacob would nowadays be called a crook. Joshua and David both committed savage atrocities upon innocent people in war; Elijah (for all that he revived the widow's son, an act that could be ascribed to a social sense of justice—"one good turn deserves another") caused to be burnt alive two separate companies of innocent soldiers obeying superior orders, and against Elisha's intervention to prevent the butchering of prisoners-of-war must be set the horrible incident of the forty-two children torn by bears. We find cases of "higher goodness" in Solomon's prayer, in David's refusal to drink the water for which men had risked their lives; in Elisha's concern for the prisoners; in the notables of Ephraim who took Oded's advice and showed pity on the captives from Judah; in Jethro's advice to Moses; in Jehosophat's charge to the judges. In all other passages where true Goodness shines through, a poet, a lawgiver or an editor of proverbial wisdom is speaking. It is in the thoughts of such men about God and righteousness, not in the acts and words ascribed to God and his servants, that I found what I was looking for. Considering the length of the Old Testament, the harvest, although of high quality, was not abundant. I discovered no more than one hundred and twenty-two passages, most of them consisting of a single verse, in which an idea of Goodness is formulated which it seems impossible to attribute to the pressures of either evolution or of society. In these passages the imagined Goodness is sheer and disinterested, if not in every case as entirely innocent of any hope of reward as was the virtue of the pagan Regulus.

My quest was a serious one, but in pursuing it I enjoyed the best of holiday reading. Many of the ancient authors of that extraordinary hotch-potch, so strangely known as the Word of God, were born story-tellers. There is vivid dialogue, the art of character-isation by a couple of strokes; economy and drama. On the verandah of an English hotel the sight of an elderly layman daily perusing his Bible, pencil in hand, would probably provoke whisperings. Few would surmise that he was merely enjoying himself. But so it was, and for those who can stomach violence and horrors and have a taste for poetry I strongly recommend the Old Testa-ment. To the modern generation, I am told, such a recommendation can be made in good faith and with-out irony.

But, to get the full savour of these writings, the reader must use the Authorised Version. I doubt whether it is possible to exaggerate the additional prestige conferred upon the old Jewish authors by the accident that the first translation into English to be widely read was made at the beginning of the seven-teenth century. You have only to contrast our own with a French Bible to appreciate what sheer beauty a language can accomplish. Indeed, the high poetic diction of our Authorised Version throws its cloak over the cruelties of Jehovah much as that of Homer covers the barbarities of Achilles. And not over the cruelties only, but over Jehovah's sheer inadequacy to make good his claims to Godhead. There can be few passages in the whole body of English poetry to equal the superb speeches in which God replies to Job "out of the whirl-wind." And yet what do they amount to? Job has posed the ultimate questions of good and evil, of undeserved suffering; and Jehovah's answer, stripped of the splendour of the rhetoric, is: (1) that Job has very little scientific knowledge; and (2) that man is a puny creature compared to a hippopotamus. Which are no answers at all.

The Old Testament writers are spread over about eight hundred years at the least and, having marked my one hundred and twenty-two passages, the next step was to arrange them, as far as possible, in chronological order, since one of the main interests in my search was to discover whether, and to what degree, there had been progress in Old Testament ethics. I do not carry in my head the opinions of modern scholars about the dates of the Old Testament writings, and had to wait until my return home, both to compare the Authorised with the Revised Version, and to place my chosen texts each in its proper century. This could be done only roughly, partly because scholars do not always agree, and partly because some of the later writers have made use of, or edited, writings of centuries before their time. Having thought it more plausible to credit the later editors with any examples of Goodness in their works, my summary may have been unjust to the older authors. (It is worth noting that no single instance of Goodness can be found in Numbers, or in the equally late-edited Books of Joshua and Judges.)

The results of my search can be summarised, by centuries B.C. and by Books, as follows (the numbers refer to the passages, mostly single verses, which exhibit a sense of higher Goodness in the writer or editor):

| | | | | | |
|---|---|---|---|---|---|
| 8th century B.C. | Amos | 2 | 7th century B.C. | Zephaniah | I |
| | Hosea | 3 | | Jeremiah | 3 |
| | Isaiah | 6 | | Deuteronomy | 9 |
| | Micah | 2 | | Habakkuk | 2 |
| | I & II Sam. | 2 | | I & II Kings | 3 |
| | | — | | | — |
| | | 15 | | | 18 |

| | | | | | |
|---|---|---|---|---|---|
| 6th century B.C. | A few Psalms | 5 | 5th century B.C. | Malachi | I |
| | Ezekiel | 4 | | Genesis | 4 |
| | II Isaiah | 14 | | Exodus | 6 |
| | Lamentations | 4 | | Leviticus | 6 |
| | Zechariah | 2 | | Job | 7 |
| | | — | | | — |
| | | 29 | | | 24 |

| | | | | | |
|---|---|---|---|---|---|
| 4th to 3rd century B.C. | Chronicles | 7 | 2nd century B.C. | Daniel | 4 |
| | Nehemiah | I | | Psalms | 18 |
| | Ecclesiastes | I | | Proverbs | 5 |
| | | — | | | — |
| | | 9 | | | 27 |

Even in these passages there is a good deal of repetition, and in a few cases one century has obviously copied from an earlier one. But when the matrix from which these pearls are gathered is considered—the prevailing violence and cruelty, the narrow racialism, the extraordinary juxtapositions of good and bad in the thoughts of the same persons (e.g. Jeremiah, Ezekiel or the Psalmists)—the pearls are surely very remarkable. It is true that the middle centuries of the first millennium B.C. (whence, except for the Psalms, the bulk of these passages are culled) saw a blossoming of human Goodness in many distant and only barely related regions. In India, in China, in Persia, in Greece, new ethics were being propounded, some of which were definitely of the non-paying, unself-regarding kind. There were even cases of minor deities springing up who preferred benevolence to power. But curiously only the Jews attempted to re-create their tribal God in the image of themselves at their best, refusing, in the light of their new and higher ethical instincts, to accept the tyrannical Deity of their own most sacred records and traditions. It was a triumph for Conscience over Authority.

Unfortunately Authority had the last word, and a priesthood that, like all priesthoods, must need conserve tradition or perish saw fit to bind up together all these histories, prophecies, poems and romances and call them the Word of God. The greater part of them are wholly irrelevant to any thoughts about Goodness or a God of Goodness. Many of them positively degrade the Deity. They have supplied authority for every kind of human vindictiveness, cruelty and enslavement. Their proper place is on the shelves reserved for belles lettres, poetry, primitive history, anthropology or comparative religion. A large proportion make perfect holiday reading, as I have said. But that it should be necessary to read through such masses of miscellaneous literature, however entertaining, in order to discover in what rare Jewish souls, and when, a love of Goodness for its own sake first blossomed would be incredible were it not true.

Outside the Roman Church and the Protestant ministries, most of the teachers and educationists of the Western world no longer regard the Old Testament as the Word of God. The old writings, because of this absurd claim made for them, are falling into neglect and disregard. If they were to be re-edited and re-grouped, the bulk of them being commended as absorbing and entertaining literature, and a few passages collected and distinguished as the record of the search, by a few wise men, of one small nation, over nearly a thousand years before Jesus, for what is required in a Deity to satisfy the human conscience at its most sensitive and exacting, these ancient books might enjoy a new prestige. The archbishops might not approve, but how many of us nowadays care for what archbishops think? To coming generations in the English-speaking world something precious might be restored, if once again that great store of common reference were at hand to enlarge their means of communicating and to make the English language at its most noble familiar to their ears.

## CHAPTER XXII

# A RUMINANT AT LARGE

THAT I happened to re-read the Old Testament on the roof of a restaurant at Lerici, and under vine-trellises, was a mere accident. I could have read it at home. But it is no accident that travels through Tuscany and Umbria compel reflections upon Christendom, as it has been and as it exists. These regions are naturally fertile; sunshine to ripen the crops never fails; grain and olives and vines all do well there. The best soil is naturally in the valleys and the miniature plains that flank and follow the course of the streams, and you would expect to find an agricultural people building their settlements and siting their farmhouses on the low ground, on the good soil itself. But you find nothing of the sort. The homes of these farming people are huddled together in walled towns on the tops of the hills, far from their fields. The steeper and higher the hill, the more certain it is to be crowned with a fortified and desperately over-crowded town or village. In the fabulous Age of Faith, to which our Bellocs turned with so curious a nostalgia, the Tuscan farmer, for his very life, had to toil up to one of these strongholds every evening: from their walls, only too often, he had to watch the ravaging of his crops by armed bands. The spectacle of these little fortress-towns, capping every rock or prominence, delights us today; they have the appearance of having perched there, with unerring taste, to beautify the landscape. But in sober fact they are the evidence of almost incredible labour and hardship forced upon the inhabitants of a fruitful land by sheer terror. Even the religious houses, the convents and the monasteries dared not, as do our northern abbeys, sit down in comfortable valleys, with their fish-ponds and good fields. They stand high, remote and waterless, for safety's sake. In the same centuries when our English monks and common people could spread themselves at large over the lands they tilled, in the main undisturbed by the feuds of kings and nobles, these Italian peasants had no respite from fear. They multiplied saints and shrines; the Virgin had her niche at every street-corner; in those congested strongholds there was, it seems, always room for another church; but the prayers, the invocations, brought no relief from rapine and bloodshed, and the Pope himself rode in armour at the head of armed men. And in this fierce and sun-drenched land the quarrels were not only between land-hungry nobles or between Emperor and Pope but between the burghers and citizens of one great city and the next—or even one small town and its neighbour. The people of little Assisi were slaughtered by the people of little Perugia on the neighbouring hill; in the following year the fellow-townsmen of St Francis took a bloody revenge. And so it went on.

To the fear of Hell, coupled with the belief in the priestly power of granting, for a consideration and a deathbed repentance, effective absolution, we are indebted, in our own country, for many of our greatest churches and abbeys. Their splendour is as often commensurate with the sins as with the piety of their

founders. In Italy it was to a different fear—that of
sudden death at the hands of a neighbour—that we owe
the aesthetic delights of the landscape, and the noble
siting of those fascinating hill-towns. When we breakfast on the terraces or balconies of the inns at San
Gimignano, at Certaldo Alto, at Montepulciano, at
Assisi, at Poppi, at Orvieto, at Urbino, or look down
from their massive walls at the immeasurable undulations of the rich farmlands, it is difficult to believe, where
all is peace and good husbandry, in the fears and
ferocities that set our breakfast-table at such a height,
with such a view. Rather one has a feeling that a romantic and artistic people hauled these great stones up the
precipitous slopes to savour such enjoyment as is ours.
But we arrived at our eyrie in a motor-bus, and a
descent on foot into the plain, to walk at ease among the
vines and olive-groves and patches of maize, soon cures
us of any such nonsense. For the view of the town-walls
from below, and the toil up the steep *salita* in the heat is
enough to convince us that no tillers of those level lands
would have laboured at that titanic masonry, or daily
groaned up those formidable slopes, for the sake of a
view or anything else in the world but sheer necessity.

Do the hankerers after the Age of Faith ever account
to themselves for the contrast between those centuries
of fear and the centuries of security that succeeded
them? War at its most destructive has twice come to
Italy in my own lifetime, and the fear that haunts the
whole world today is a possibility so monstrous that it
will in all probability compel us to keep the peace; but
these wars and this fear have been of another kind, and
from quite other causes, than those that once changed
the Italian landscape. Between the wars, and after them,

the Italian peasants, at any rate in northern Italy, have fallen back into the old friendly ways of the unlocked door and the unhedged vineyard. And for these they must thank not the Faith, but the men of the Enlightenment; the jurists and political thinkers and moralists of the seventeenth and eighteenth centuries, the new compassion, the enlarged sympathies, of the humanists of the nineteenth. Free-ranging thought and a new conception of liberty, not the Faith, put the hill-towns out of date: these former preservers of life itself have declined, gracefully and perhaps gratefully, into the merely picturesque. And it is not to be forgotten that the last surviving region of corruption and oppression was that of the Papal States.

The Faith itself survives, gentle, pervasive, but unobtrusive. The charm of a Woman-Goddess, herself humble and approachable, has, to judge from appearances, much to do with its survival. In every Italian church, great and small, it is at her shrine or side-chapel that the candles are massed and the worshippers kneel. Sometimes a local saint of great renown, such as St Francis or St Antony, is given the preference, but in general the Virgin has no rival. Few kneel before the High Altar, the crucified Christs in the side-chapels get no attention if a Virgin is at hand. And at hand she always is, often multiplied, but not equal, in her several simulacra, in honour. One Virgin, in a church of many, has invariably the supremacy. And after her, a saint. Dogmatically, of course, the Virgin is no goddess, and her worshippers, if pressed, would undoubtedly agree. Her function, *de fide*, is intercession, and the very foundation of her attraction for worshippers is her humanity and consequent capacity for fellow-feeling,

14+

especially with women. But a moment's reflection upon her present celestial functions leads to the inescapable conclusion that either she possesses the unimaginable faculties of a god, or it is of no use to beg for her intercession. For the prayers made to her, at every minute of the twenty-four hours, must run into hundreds of thousands, and an intelligence that could register and distinguish those multitudinous messages, pass them on to her Son or to His Father, receive Their answers and re-transmit them to her petitioners must be a god's intelligence, so far removed from anything remotely conceivable by a human brain that to claim humanity, in any known sense, for its possessor is absurd. The same argument holds good, in a lesser degree, for the busiest of the saints. They, too, must have developed faculties so super-human as to be more godlike than manlike. Whatever theology may say, the Virgin and some of the greater women saints must, if they truly function, be goddesses, and the Italian women, at any rate of the peasant and the humbler sorts, may be regarded as unconscious polytheists. I say 'women' because although a large percentage of the congregations at a Sunday Mass is composed of men, you rarely see a man kneeling, as the women kneel every day of the week, at a Virgin's shrine. Perhaps the most striking thing about the Italians in church is their easy and offhand behaviour in what Protestants call the "sacred edifice." They appear to have no feelings of awe, or even of what we should call reverence; in the greater churches they walk about freely during the sermon and even chat together; a Sunday School at Sarzana was all giggles, unrebuked; and in S. Agostino at Montepulciano I saw two little servitors, in surplices and lace, having a desperate and furious bout of fisticuffs all over the echoing church. But the culmination of insouciance was reached in the Church of St Francis at La Verna, that high and holy place where the saint received the stigmata. It was at a festa in his honour, and Mass was being said at the three altars simultaneously. The large congregation wandered about the church continuously, talking among themselves, and at the altar before which we stood, the priest himself bandied remarks over his shoulder to acquaintances in the crowd, while actually performing the elaborate and symbolic gestures of worship. From their appearance of apathy and indifference the officiating clergy might have been Tibetan monks turning a prayer-wheel. But everything at La Verna, except the exquisite Della Robbia terra-cottas, was a sore disappointment. For many hundreds of yards all round the church and monastery the ground is stained and disfigured by rotting litter, left by the coach-loads of pilgrims and sightseers. That the monks are aware of this revolting mess was clear, for several of them were sitting among the débris, smoking cigarettes and talking to their friends. But they were indifferent to it, for the accumulation was not of days, but of months, possibly of years. St Francis was one of the most remarkable figures in the history of Christendom; one does not need to be of the Roman faith to appreciate a man so singular that he alone excelled his own Master in charity. For whereas Jesus was capable of violent vituperation when provoked by such play-acting as we witnessed at the festival service, it seems certain that St Francis, after his conversion, could have been harsh to no man. His attempt to prefer the spirit to the letter of Christianity failed: the Church saw to that; but his courage and selflessness were extraordinary and, sanctity apart, a place so indubitably linked with his life as La Verna should be cherished, not soiled and neglected. Italian towns and villages nowadays are conspicuously clean and tidy; their public squares and gardens are free of litter, and we were astonished at the speed and thoroughness with which the great cloisters at Ascoli and the piazza at Certaldo were scoured and cleaned after a market and a cattle-show. So that it is all the more surprising that the monks of La Verna should tolerate such squalor.

Whether to credit the influence of the gentle goddess, or some innate grace of this Latin race, with the good manners, the cheerfulness, and the apparent contentment of the country and small-town people of northern Italy, I do not know. But they are a friendly lot, and the health and good-humour of the children is especially conspicuous. The sunshine may play its part; possibly the drinking of wine has something to do with it. Their one great blemish is their passion for noise, which the coming of the Vespa, that devilish motor-bicycle, has enabled them to gratify as never before. These machines have no silencers; indeed, so an Italian lady assured me, the young people pay several extra pounds to have amplifiers fitted to them. I remember two boys at Narni who spent an entire evening racing one of these machines up and down the narrow canyon-like street not to get anywhere but for the sake of the clatter, like that of fifty machine-guns, which reverberated from the cliff-like houses. And everybody seemed to enjoy it. In the exquisite Piazza of Bassano, where we had looked forward to drinking in the beauty of that ancient place together with our *stregas*, four separate loudspeakers blared out the radio-programmes from four cafés. In little arcaded Poppi a television-van stood before the miniature domed church and shattered the night with grotesque and discordant bellowings, and the whole population assembled, bringing chairs from their houses, to enjoy the ear-splitting clamour. In Florence, where the streets are narrow, conversation is impossible; in Rome, where the streets are broader, you can hear the voice of a companion if he shouts. No wonder we tend nowadays to drift to Venice.

This love of noise for its own sake can at times give to a visitor the impression that he is among barbarians; that this ancient home of civilisation has been once again overrun by savages; one's nervous reaction is to be violent, sweeping, and contemptuous of such a people. And then sitting, say, in the red-brick cloisters, built before St Francis was born, of the Osteria del Vicario at Certaldo Alto, looking down upon the many-coloured Tuscan landscape, after being welcomed and waited upon, and made much of by the jovial inn-keeping brothers and their families, you repent of your irritation, and decide that in kindliness and good manners these Italians are pre-eminent. Cheerful, un-grasping and obliging, our hosts, who did all the work of the place themselves, gave to their paid services the warmth of hospitality and to their farewells the accent of friendship. Nothing could be more civilised than the fashions of this unpretending inn.

The taxi-driver at Sarzana, after dropping us at the foot of the broad steps that lead up to the principal church, asked us what it was that drew us foreign visitors to these antiquated fanes, when so many fine modern buildings were available. Even had we had the Italian in which to explain, which we had not, I doubt

14*

if he would have understood, for a people who can line
the highroad from Milan to Bergamo with advertise-
ments the size of a house, at hundred-yard intervals,
on both sides of the road, for a distance of forty miles,
or deface the peerless arcades of the Certosa at Ferrara
with horrifying monuments, must have lost all sense
of beauty. But when did they lose it? At Volterra the
infuriating vandalism which has blocked up the double
arcades of a most rare eleventh-century cloister, and
concealed the whole southern wall of the exquisite
twelfth-century Duomo with mean dwellings, is itself
venerable, two hundred years old at least. In England,
in spite of early examples such as the dreadful thirteenth-
century "corona" in honour of Becket which ruined
Canterbury's exquisite Norman apse, it is fairly easy to
date the general loss of "eye" for proportion and fitness
in buildings: it perished with the Regency. Italy, from
all appearances, was spared a Gothic revival, and probably, from lack of prosperity, built little or nothing
during the nineteenth century. There is nothing in their
larger cities to compare with the unbridled vulgarity
of London's great shopping-streets, or the fussy falsity
of a Pont Street or Cadogan Square. Their suburbs can
be plain and monotonous to the point of dreariness, but
they are not showy or pretentious, and their sober
dullness in a way enhances the pleasure of suddenly
turning a corner and finding oneself face to face with
some miracle in brick or stone, or, more often, a whole
group, a piazza-full, of such wonders. I really have
gasped, audibly, on a first sight of such perfection, often
contrived through four or more centuries, as can be
seen in the main square at Ascoli, the Piazza della Loggia
at Brescia, the group of Sangallo palaces at the top of

Montepulciano, the miniature piazzas at Pienza and Norcia, the cluster of buildings at Todi, and the great Palladian Basilica, flanked by the slender, soaring twelfth-century clock-tower, in the Piazza dei Signori at Vicenza. The men who, from the twelfth century onwards, added church or arcade or town hall to these close-knit groups had an unerring instinct for the whole, when adding, in however novel a style, some additional part. There is infinite diversity, but there is always harmony.

Today the "Jolly" hotels are everywhere going up, all glass and concrete, regardless of their surroundings. And as far as that goes who are we—or indeed any modern nation—to criticise? We lost our sense of proportion a hundred and fifty years ago, and have no right to complain. All the same, there was something disturbing about the conversation of the good-looking young man in the café at Montepulciano. Seeing that we were English, he came across to our table for a chat, for he spoke excellent English himself. He was a local landowner, he told us, but when we congratulated him on living in that incomparable countryside, he shrugged his shoulders. Did we know Liverpool? Ah, that was the place for him. He had spent a year there, a truly splendid city. How he longed to return! But he was tied by the leg in this remote, uninteresting place by his property and his duties. As none of us knew Liverpool, we were in no position to contradict him when he assured us, with sparkling black eyes, that Montepulciano, commanding a view of half Tuscany, is not a patch on it. We murmured politely that our next holiday, perhaps, must be a trip to Liverpool. But we felt, uneasily, that in one kind of sensibility this educated, well-bred young man was on a level with the taxi-driver of Sarzana.

To travel in Italy where all the arts, including most of the architecture, were mainly inspired by the Christian faith is to be daily compelled to reflect upon that, and all other, religions. And it does not take long to discover that, once the great and sanguinary struggle between Reformers and Counter-reformers had petered out in the seventeenth century, the majority of Christians ceased to be concerned with the proofs and arguments for their beliefs, and were content with the faith in which they happened to be born. I imagine that ninety-nine per cent of the followers of the world's religions, in West and East alike, believe what they believe because their fathers believed it. The one per cent are those who, after study and thought, either acquire genuine conviction or change their creed for another. This leads to the curious reflection that had the Arch-bishop of Canterbury been born a Catholic, or a Tibetan, he would undoubtedly have become a promi-nent Roman Catholic dignitary or a Buddhist Abbot. Had the present Pope been a child of the manse, he might well have been, today, the Moderator of the Church Assembly in Scotland. Both, like their respec-tive flocks, were caught young, baptised while still unconscious, instructed, catechised, confirmed and impressed, consciously and subconsciously, with the "truth" of a set of beliefs whose foundations their training and natural piety have made it impossible for them to question. To an onlooker—and no doubt to the Supreme Onlooker—there is something absurd in the idea that our beliefs on the greatest of all problems are settled for us by the accident of birth. But the believers see nothing odd in it; on the contrary, they take great pride in the hereditary aspect of their faith, and in the great Prayer Book Debate of 1928 there were loud cheers for Sir Edward Carson when he declared in the House of Commons that what he had learnt at his mother's knee was good enough for him. But archbishops who, but for an accident, might have been Buddhists, and Popes who could well have been Lutherans, can hardly be surprised if our onlooker pays no attention to what they affirm to be the Will of God in every sort of question, large and small, and prefers to hammer it out for himself, if such Will there be. And the first step in such hammering will probably be an attempt to see things in proper proportion. And when the duration of life on this planet is considered, beside which the whole history of Man is but an instant, the onlooker, seeking for the Will of God, has to look for signs of that Will during countless aeons before men existed at all. And not only that, but during the infinitely greater and quite ungraspable period when there was not merely no life on this planet but no planet; what sort of God presided then, and what was His Will? To see evidence of any moral or emotional qualities—such as Love, which a New Testament author pronounced to be God's essence—is as impossible as to imagine a Trinity presiding over, and manipulating, a universe consisting principally of hydrogen. Nor are those qualities easily discernible even in the fraction of time during which life, but not man, has existed on this planet. In the sanguinary evolutionary struggle, with its apparent concern for the species but never for the individual, it is possible to find evidence of purpose and direction, but none of emotional or moral motives.

Consummate artistry, almost inexplicable without an artist, is also apparent, but it is art for art's sake, the work of an artist without compassion. No faintest indication is there, in all that incalculable immensity of time and space, of love, or pity, or goodness, or self-sacrifice, until the appearance of Man. It is man, and only man, who has loved, who has laughed, who has been unselfish, who has distinguished right from wrong.

How did man, himself physically a product of evolution, an animal whose driving impulses were to eat, to reproduce and to survive, acquire his conscience, his capacity for selflessness, his sense of humour, his altruism? To me, the humblest of onlookers, there is only one explanation: that at some point in his short history Man's animal organism was taken possession of, colonised as it were, by some Intelligence from without, itself endowed with the emotions, the moral sense, which distinguishes us from the rest of the animal kingdom and makes us, as Sir Julian Huxley points out, unique. That this source of our humanity was also the creator of the hydrogen-universe and the director of the daily massacres we find in nature I suspect to be highly unlikely. I prefer to regard it as a moral Intelligence, engaged in warfare against cruelty, indifference and suffering; the enemy, not the creator, of all noxious things, a fighting champion of goodness, but very far from being Almighty. This hypothesis of a colonising Intelligence is made more plausible for myself by my conviction, based on evidence, of our survival of death with our memories, personalities and wills intact. The existence of human individuals in a disembodied state is an argument for the like existence of moral and intelligent being far superior to ourselves. I see no necessity to presuppose only supernatural or non-material (so-called "spiritual") conditions for such an existence. The discovery that all matter is energy, and recent experiments in telepathy, seem to leave plenty of room for such an existence within this self-same universe with which our scientists are concerned.

My theory of an extra-evolutionary source of our moral consciousness and of our capacity for love and self-sacrifice cannot make any positive contribution to the supreme problem of whether a personal God exists, and of what His attributes may be. The sheer babyhood of the human race against the background of incalculable time makes anything but a questing agnosticism absurdly presumptuous. Even our infantile religious faiths were formulated at a time when, from lack of knowledge, their founders were, by comparison with ourselves, like an infant whose universe is bounded by the four walls of the nursery compared with a grown-up who leaves the house to gaze at some wide view. The grown-up no longer, like the child in the cradle, gives to his God the attributes of Nanny, but his wider view brings him greater, not less, perplexities. All the same, the possession of a conscience does enable us to reach a few negative conclusions, to be persuaded of certain things that a personal God, if goodness be one of His attributes, cannot be. He can hardly, for example, be Almighty, since He has patently not yet won the battle against the cruelties and suffering that pervade the natural world. He cannot be arbitrary and unjust, as He must be if He distinguishes between baptised and un-baptised infants. And He cannot have fully revealed Himself, as Christianity claims, to a race not out of swaddling clothes, incapable of imagining a Being greater than one with the powers, the bounties, and the uncertain temper of a Nanny.

We men have, hitherto, made and re-made gods in our own image, and it is hard to see what else, in our infancy which still continues, we could have done. Unfortunately the images we set up in babyhood have been fixed and frozen by the various faiths. A great part of mankind no longer accepts them. But the trouble is that so long as the faiths persist in worshipping their own imperfect, childish artifacts the majority who reject them become disposed, in their revulsion, to wash their hands of the whole subject. And this is, surely, a betrayal and a breach of trust in a race of creatures so highly privileged as ourselves. If God is, in our image, still unknowable, at least we have conscience enough to recognise Goodness. And in pursuing that we might, who knows, at least deserve, if not achieve, further enlightenment.

I have mentioned a sense of humour as an attribute of humanity that seems, like conscience and the rest, to have come from an "outside" source. And for much of my life, when my God was still a Person and inevitably endowed by me, like everybody else's, with human qualities, I have been accustomed, privately, to judge much of human behaviour by the criterion of whether or not it was likely to "make God laugh." (Curiously enough, much as I enjoy laughter, I never wanted God to enjoy it; if I felt that a thing would "make God laugh" I condemned it.) And the sort of things that I felt must be laughable in God's sight were, not unnaturally, those which most closely concerned Himself. Praising Him, for instance; praying to Him with "vain repetitions"; dressing up for Him; dividing

Him into Three Persons; making Him the author of the Bible; deifying and equating with Him a young Jewish genius, whose unique wisdom and moral insight have, fortunately for the world, been able to transcend theology; thanking Him for bad harvests, asserting that our children's deaths from preventable diseases are "His Will"; and a hundred other absurdities which often belittle, and sometimes insult, One whose mind, it can be safely said, is unlikely to have anything in common with the minds of theologians born in the first few seconds of man's existence on this small planet.

Although, with increasing years, I no longer have the presumption to humanise the Source of Conscience (for I can go no further in speculation) to the extent of hearing Its laughter, I find myself no longer condemning, but rather sharing, what I imagined to be "God's" amusement at the goings-on of the various Churches. And an indulgent and even sympathetic amusement it is, largely brought about, I suspect, by my wanderings in Italy. For whereas the sight of an Anglican bishop, in spite of his rather absurd hat and gaiters, can only excite compassion for his laborious and harassed life of dedication to a set of beliefs which I hold to be baseless, the sight of an Italian priest whirring up the cobbled streets of Urbino on a Vespa, cassock flying, is delightful. For the priest is not harassed; not for him, as for the Anglican bishop, the agonising questions such, for example, as the legitimacy of contraceptives in a world made wretched by over-population; he is under authority; all moral questions are decided for him; his functions are specific, precise and make no demands upon his reason or his conscience. Indeed the Roman Church, in a Latin country, is essentially a cheerful

15

institution, with the cheerfulness that comes from self-assurance. Italy contains Communists and declared infidels in numbers far exceeding those in these islands, but they are invisible to the traveller, whereas the Church, with her festivals and processions and Saints and Virgins, is ubiquitous, gay, and self-confident. Although her pomp, her splendour and her pragmatic polytheism would have astonished and dismayed the young prophet of Galilee whom she prefers to portray as a child in his Mother's arms, they enliven and refresh the laborious days of the peasants and the poor, and when contrasted with the drab ugliness of our own village bethels and tabernacles, or even with the cold interiors of our churches built for a more decorative cult, the Italian churches have, undeniably, a more winning way with them. For an onlooker, liberated from his inherited Protestantism, and persuaded that all theologies are presumptuous and infantile attempts to define the unknowable, there is a charm about the "façade" of the Roman religion, at any rate beneath Italian skies, which accords with the beauty of the palpable façades in brick or in marble of the churches themselves. And in an age when Rome has abandoned for good the inquisitions and persecutions of the past there is nothing to shudder at, and much to enjoy, in the spectacle of her ancient and unchanging ritual. Her beliefs, even her superstitions, did after all inspire the greatest visual art yet known; she was the conserver of beauty and letters throughout the Dark Ages; and, hotly as she would deny it, she remains and may she long remain, a superb monument to the divinity of Man. For in spite of my hesitation to use a word whose true meaning I am incapable of grasping, there seems no other word than "divine" to describe the mysterious source of these "immortal longings," that passion for beauty and goodness, that capacity for self-sacrifice, which distinguish us, in spite of our many iniquities, from all other living creatures.

"The greatest art yet known" may seem a bold thing to assert in the face of the Greeks, but the Greeks, having achieved perfection of its kind, soon became unadventurous and repetitive, whereas Christianity, whether in building, painting or sculpture, continued over a thousand years to inspire originality and experiment. And in Italy you have the whole astonishing variety— with the one exception of the more resplendent Gothic —before your eyes. The Greeks, you feel, would have been content with the perfection of Torcello or Ravenna, and happy enough to reproduce it indefinitely. But the peoples of Italy, invigorated, it is true, by Gothic, Lombard and Norman conquerors, were continuously spurred on by the piety or repentances of their great men to go one better than their forefathers, and the wonder is that they succeeded. Not, perhaps, in actually excelling their predecessors, since there is to be found perfection of its kind in every century except the nineteenth, but in making fresh combinations, new arrangements of arch and line and curve, in rediscovering and adapting classic forms and adornments. So that in every considerable city and town you find them, cheek by jowl, churches and baptisteries from earliest Romanesque to Palladian and Baroque, exquisite or resplendent, but invariably triumphant from the point of view of their designers. And the faith that inspired them all was the venerable, unchanging faith of Rome.

As for the painters and sculptors, they were fortunate indeed in the subject-matter provided for them by that Faith. Not for them the awe of Allah which restricted Moslem artists to arabesques and geometrical patterns. Having raised to godhead a human being, of whose life on earth a vivid record remains, their creed enabled them to depict their God Himself against a background of all that was most familiar and acceptable to their fellow-believers. And they had the inestimable boon of the Virgin Mary, gentle, innocent, awestruck, maternal, compassionate, on whom to lavish all that their hearts and imaginations could contrive in the way of grace and beauty. It is true that the pagans had an Athene, a Diana or an Aphrodite as models, but these goddesses had not even, like Apollo, dwelt with Admetus or known the touch and taste, the warm proximity, of ordinary earthly things. Mary had been a living girl in Palestine, and the painters of the Renaissance, reacting against the stylised, Byzantine, icon-like treatment of her by the primitives, found ample authority in the Gospel stories for painting her as a human woman, in human surroundings. In their own eyes they must have been as much historical as devotional painters; the Annunciations, the Nativities, the Flights into Egypt, were no less imagined portrayals of actual events than were our nineteenth-century paintings of Raleigh spreading his cloak before Queen Elizabeth I. Nor did the painter hesitate to take living women as their models; the fair delicacy of Fra Lippo Lippi's Virgins had belonged to his mistress, Lucrezia Buti; and if chivalry and devotion for the most part called for a patrician, high-bred look in the Mother of God, there are many Virgins, scarcely less appealing, for whom peasant or country girls may well have sat. The one touch of realism that could not, in that age, be permitted was to portray Mary as in face she was: a Jewess; and the same is true of her Son. Jewish types, oriental costumes, palm-trees and camels were familiar enough to these Renaissance painters, and freely used for the High Priests and Pharisees and crowds in their Trials and Scourgings and Crucifixions; but the Jews were a race of outcasts, damned from birth, and Christ, his Mother and His disciples were invariably given the features and colouring of western, not Semitic, peoples. Nor were the painters concerned with historical backgrounds. It was the familiar Italian scene that they painted; the hills, the soil, the trees, the little towns, the white oxen of Umbria or Tuscany as we see them today; and this must have been deliberately done, so as to bring home to the spectator, by the vivid presentation of all that was most familiar, a sense of the truth and actuality of the scenes depicted. No liberty was too great to take if it pleased the patron or attracted the spectator; Montefeltro's broken nose is present, in bronze, at the taking down of Christ's body from the Cross, and, in paint, at the Last Supper; and the painters liked to include their own self-portraits among the well-known figures whose presence at biblical scenes must have lent an air of authority, a kind of guarantee, to the artist's representation.

The choice of subject-matter for these paintings was narrow enough, and the Nativities and Annunciations are endlessly repeated, but that does not matter. The number of these painters who had a fresh eye for a well-worn theme is extraordinary; besides, they enjoyed experiment, and had the spur of competition, not only among themselves but among their patrons, the great nobles or religious houses. They were picture-making for a small, well-informed and highly critical circle of spectators; their pictures were bespoken, and there was no starving in garrets for these artists, no pressure from dealers "to please the public"; they could take their time and do the best they knew. The result for us, four hundred years later, is that in spite of the everlasting recurrence of the same subjects we do not grow weary of them, but are charmed, exhilarated and refreshed.

In crediting the Faith with the inspiration of so much beauty, I am not forgetting the Bacchuses and Venuses and Centaurs of a Titian or a Botticelli, the pastorals of a Giorgione, or the palaces and villas of a Sangallo or a Palladio. Patrons and artists alike were often worldly-minded men, Popes and prelates included, and religion had no monopoly of art. But upon a wanderer about Italy the overwhelming impression is of the pervasiveness and ubiquity of the Roman Faith, and of the splendour and variety of its achievements. There is no need to be "religious" or a believer to enjoy all this loveliness. But its main source has a right to be recognised. I do not know what effect so much richness has upon the minds of our young painters and architects and sculptors. Perhaps they have not seen it. For the architects, should they happen to see it and to be moved to emulation, the dilemma is a sad one, since the materials are beyond any patron's purse, and the craftsmen to shape them no longer exist. And the young painters and sculptors, finding all the pictures and sculpture to be "representations," will have to be bold indeed to approve of anything so out of fashion.

I am not myself old-fashioned enough to condemn semi-representational painting where deliberate

distortions are employed, or even wholly abstract art.
El Greco was an early pioneer in distortion of the human
figure, and used it with magical effect. I can admire
Modigliani. I enjoy Christopher Wood's tottering pink
villas, and Dufy's airy, unsubstantial waterfronts. I find
Matisse enchanting. I am immensely moved by Henry
Moore's three mysterious, microcephalic presences in
Battersea Park. And as for pure abstractions I see no
reason, in principle, why a painter may not attempt to
do, with colours, what a musician does with sounds.
Music is the first of all arts, and is wholly unrepre-
sentational. We constantly use musical terms for the
description of a painting, speaking of tones, harmonies,
rhythm and the like. Why is a painter to be laughed at
if he attempts, with colours and outlines, to construct
something as harmonious, as shapely, as a piece of
music? Klee has done it and Braque has done it: to name
but two who happen to have given me personal
pleasure. Texture alone has a most subtle power of
pleasing. It is a form of orchestration.

No, although I think abstract paintings should be
called "compositions" rather than "pictures," I believe
them to be a legitimate and fascinating form of art.
But it is a form full of perils for the young artist. It
looks so easy. It appears, unlike music or drawing, to
have no grammar to be mastered. That its successful
practitioners have been masters of the traditional tech-
niques of drawing and painting seems to be overlooked.
As a result, coxcombs do throw the contents of their
palettes in the face of the public and ask for applause,
or twist up a piece of wire into any old shape and
consider themselves a Henry Moore. The old repre-
sentational painters had to learn their craft, painfully,

before they achieved the skill to communicate to the
spectator their individual, original and often exciting
vision. For any kind of communication to succeed, to
"get across," there must be a common term of reference.
To the old painters natural objects supplied that common term; the spectator, beginning with simple
recognition, was led on to share that fresh eye for things
which artists have and we have not.

I do not think it will do for the young wire-twisters
and colour-splashers to reply that I have just likened
abstract art to music, and that musicians can hardly be
said to communicate with their audience by reference to
some natural objects. For the sound-waves which, in
any given age and region, happen to please the contemporary human ear are as much natural objects, only less
well organised, as mountains or nudes. It is because the
ear recognises and accepts such noises as "musical" that
the composer can "get across" the products of his own
imaginative manipulations of this raw material. But
experience has shown that there is an immense amount
of grammar, a complicated technique, to be mastered
before the composer can hope to make his manipulations
acceptable. And a young painter whose ambition it is to
charm us with his abstractions would do well to copy
Velasquez for ten years before he makes his first attempt.
I have friends of my own age, with far more knowledge
than is mine both of pictures and of the methods of
painters, who steadfastly refuse to see any merit in
painting later than that of the French Impressionists. I
detect pain in the eyes which they so swiftly avert from
the Christopher Woods and Winifred Nicholsons on
my walls. Their eyebrows rise when I let out that, were
I a Greek shipowner, I should fill my great halls with

Matthew Smiths. Nor can they understand how it is that, with so little taste, I can yet share their own enthusiasm for the great classic masters. No doubt they dismiss me as one of those Philistines who "know what they like." Well, I do know what I like, and so, if they are honest with themselves, do they. Aristotle, who thought things out, decided that the whole purpose of a work of art was to give pleasure. I am the last man to say either that taste cannot be cultivated and improved by study or that there are no standards of excellence in art. The analysis of any work of great art reveals principles and rules, and we are able to say that their observance gives us pleasure, and their neglect gives us none. But why their observance gives pleasure is a mystery; we only know, from our delight in them, that they do. It is something in our own make-up which accepts or rejects; all the same, in talking of taste, we have to remember that our own make-up is largely conditioned by our century and our hemisphere. A Chinaman enjoys noises which to us are hideous, and vice-versa. Even if we speak of such a thing as structural truth in architecture—our satisfaction in feeling that the arch or the beam will support the weight above it and not collapse—that truth depends upon the material used. Buildings in steel and concrete have quite other "principles" than those of bricks or stone. "Proportion" is a famous source of pleasure, but there is no proportion at all in *The Brothers Karamazov*. None the less it ranks high as a work of art. We praise "restraint" in, say, a Greek temple or the Redentore Church in Venice, and then find ourselves enchanted with the riotous lack of restraint in Baroque or Rococo figures, façades or decoration. The seeking for principles by which to judge a work of art can even, I believe, result in a loss of much delight. As I grow older, I find myself every year enlarging my capacity for enjoyment, largely, I think, through abandoning the critical standards of my earlier days. Only quite latterly would I have as much as glanced at the Spanish Baroque Virgin in the corner of San Nicolo on the Zattere; now I find her infinitely pleasing. And there is a wooden pulpit in the Pieta, all green and gold and curlicues and volutes—but I am not writing a guide-book. My point is that our own personal capacities for being delighted can go on expanding and if the delight comes, it is better to enjoy it than to be shocked by it. We are sometimes told that we can learn to accept novelties in art by conscientiously trying to understand what the artist himself is attempting to express. It is a fair-minded thing to do, no doubt, but I do not think it works. If the artist has failed to please, what he had in mind when at work is of no interest. If he does please, that is enough: again, his thoughts and intentions do not matter to us. Indeed, we are often the better without them: an outstanding example is *The Ring*. Wagner's music is enchanting; the words and thoughts that the composer believed himself to be expressing are preposterous. The same can be said of *The Magic Flute*. If what I am confessing to is nothing but a senile degeneration in "taste," a sad abandonment of my earlier standards, I can only recommend other elderly persons to mislay a few of their own. Life is short, and any trick for increasing the pleasures of our declining years is worth learning. But, oddly enough, I am not conscious of degeneration, or of admiring the second-rate. My enjoyment of the recognised masters is as keen as ever, and if I no longer judge modern work by comparing it with the old, I still feel—perhaps it is an illusion—that I intuitively reject the cheap, the meretricious and the shoddy. And in some respects I find myself hopelessly old-fashioned. I have so profound a conviction that, for domestic architecture on a moderate scale, the Carolean, William and Mary, and Georgian styles achieved perfection, that I would be content to see them copied and repeated again and again. Provided, of course, that the copies are true ones. One sees innumerable "Georgian" or "Queen Anne" houses go up which, from lack of attention to "proportion," or to such details as inserting the window-frames flush with the walls, miss the whole point of the originals, and give pain, not pleasure. To be in favour of "imitation" in building is, of course, a dreadful heresy to young architects, whose ambition it is to express "themselves," or "the spirit of the age," or at any rate to be "original." All the same, if one of them was able to reproduce a small Queen Anne dwelling-house with exactitude, he would need to be a master of his craft.

My thoughts have strayed like lost sheep in this chapter, but one of the inevitable results of wandering about a country like Italy is that the traveller's mind is also set meandering. Physically, you come home from "going abroad," and the voice of the first English porter at Dover, the taste of the first cup of tea in the low-swung train, give a curious, even reluctant, sense of reassurance that can only mean that you are still incorrigibly insular at heart. But mentally you can never wholly come home; you have been too much astonished and delighted, have made too close an acquaintance with the past, for that. The mere thought of a Pope leads straight to metaphysics; the sight of a walled town huddled on a hill reminds you of "old, unhappy far-off things"; the enjoyment of a Bellini makes you wonder how on earth you can take pleasure in a Gauguin, still less a Picasso. And to write about going abroad with no mention of the thoughts occasioned by your travels is to tell only half the story.

# ENVOI

I LEARNT the other day, from a lecture by Mr F. L. Lucas, that the *Anti-Jacobin* once apologised for not reporting Erskine in full because the printer had run out of capital I's. The resources of modern printing-presses are greater, and if I made this excuse for bringing my memories to an end I should not be believed, for all my inordinate use of that capital letter. The truth is that I have run out of memories, or rather, I should say, of memories that I choose to make public. What goes deepest with us, the roots of our felicity or our griefs, are not for printing. But since I have written for my own enjoyment, I confess to a pang on having done. I ought, perhaps, to apologise for all those I's. I remember the phrase "fiercely egotistical" used by the reviewer of a far better writer than I could hope to be. But I am not sure that the reviewer was fair. Personally, my pleasure in any book is heightened, not diminished, when the author puts himself into it; even in the writing of history I prefer a point of view, a touch of warmth or indignation, to the dispassionate chill of some modern historians. And if other readers agree with me, and feel that nothing comes so much to life in a book as the author's own view of things, they will not mind those I's. It is in the things that have interested me that I have tried to interest them, not in myself.

But to make things interesting, especially things that are not exotic or far-fetched but within the common run of experience, a point of view is essential. And a point of view requires an "I."

Well, as I have said, I am sorry to have done, and I should like to believe that a few readers will be sorry too.